A JOURNEY
THROUGH
SOUTH-EAST
ENGLAND

LEWES
TO
WOOLWICH

Brian J. Rance

The Book Guild Ltd

First published in Great Britain in 2020 by
The Book Guild Ltd
9 Priory Business Park
Wistow Road, Kibworth
Leicestershire, LE8 0RX
Freephone: 0800 999 2982
www.bookguild.co.uk
Email: info@bookguild.co.uk
Twitter: @bookguild

Typeset in Adobe Garamond Pro

Printed and bound in Great Britain by CPI Group (UK) Ltd, Croydon, CR0 4YY

ISBN 978 1913208 370

British Library Cataloguing in Publication Data.
A catalogue record for this book is available from the British Library.

Contents

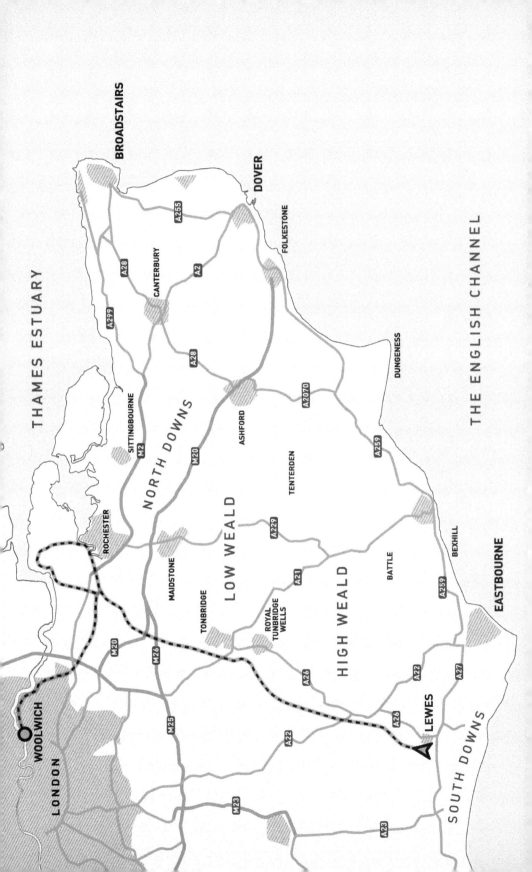

Introduction

Having completed my intended trek from Broadstairs to Lewes, passing through the county towns of both Kent and East Sussex – namely Canterbury and Lewes – and producing a book about this epic journey, I was determined to carry on walking. Returning to south-east England in the last week of August 2016, I wanted to hike back into Kent after having spent a couple of years exploring East Sussex. I imagined walking northwards from Lewes along the valley of the Sussex Ouse and up across the wild upland of Ashdown Forest to Hartfield. Toying with the Wealdway, I hoped to continue to Fordcombe, Speldhurst and Southborough, just north of Tunbridge Wells. Then, pressing ever northwards, I would visit Bidborough and Hildenborough, Shipbourne and Ightham, before scaling the North Downs scarp slope. Finally, sliding down to the Thames Estuary, I intended to pass through Stansted, Meopham, Cobham and Strood before ending up at Upnor on the Medway Estuary. The significance of Upnor in this respect is that I had resolved to return here having failed to reach this point on a previous ramble around the Hoo Peninsula in the summer of 2005 recounted in my first book. I am pleased to report that I achieved this ambition by the autumn of 2017 and the following narrative, in Chapters 1 and 2, is an account of that thoroughly enjoyable journey. In 2018, I continued walking on along the North Kent coast, eventually ending up in Woolwich, my birthplace, in the spring of 2019, recorded in Chapter 3. This, my fourth walking/companion guidebook, recounts the complete journey from Lewes to Woolwich.

1: Lewes to Hartfield

I broke my drive down from Birmingham for lunch in the pleasant Surrey village of Old Oxted, after a frustrating passage around the interminable M25. I got chatting to the barmaid in the George Inn there, who had just completed a creative writing course and was trying to write a story. I tried not to put her off in recounting my own painful experiences of writing my previous three books and the traumas of trying to get them published. The big road, the A25, now bypasses the original centre of Oxted and the narrow High Street, which was on the original cross-country route, still has some distinguished buildings. The expanded settlement of Oxted and the adjoining settlement of Limpsfield form a large urban area just over the border in Surrey on the Greensand Ridge, the equivalent of Sevenoaks in Kent. The towns are a major commuter location on the main line to London Victoria. The main justification for including this incursion into East Surrey in this narrative is that it is nearby to the source of the River Eden, a major tributary of the River Medway, Kent's river, in the vicinity of Titsey. There have been many occasions over the years when I have paused in my headlong rush down to the Kent coast in Clacket Lane service station on the M25 and observed the little archaeology display by the much-frequented toilets showing Roman remains dug up in the vicinity of Titsey, while waiting for a female companion to emerge from within. I thought one day it would be good to walk through this area, down from Beckenham, a suburb of south-east London, which used to be in the county of Kent, out past Biggin Hill and across Limpsfield Common and on back into Kent. But that perambulation would have to wait for another day!

I drove on southwards through Surrey and got hopelessly lost on unfamiliar roads, ending up in Lingfield High Street. Reorienting myself,

I passed out by the famous race course, having not realised it was there. I'm not a follower of the races but the manicured acres devoted to equine pursuits stridently announced themselves from the road as if it were a theme park. I noticed that down here the weather was hot, the long grass having changed colour from green to golden brown, unlike Birmingham, where the grass was definitely greener and the climate more like a mild winter. The harvest here was in full swing. I followed my nose, driving south-east; managing to locate Edenbridge and back on familiar ground, I proceeded southwards along the extremely useful and direct B2026.

I had another stop at the Anchor Inn in Hartfield, a venue that I had frequented on many occasions and to which I was to return to later in this journey. It was in this pleasant village that I used to shack up when visiting my publishers when they were located in Brighton, driving back and forwards across the wild expanse of Ashdown Forest. I remember on one January night, before the pub was improved, there was no heating in my room, and I simply slept in my clothes. Also, I was here one evening when my brother phoned me with the news that my mother had finally succumbed and been taken into hospital, never to emerge. Thus I have a sort of fondness for this pub, desperately needing investment to renovate its splendid, ornate, rotting veranda, which I admired immensely. If I was a retired, skilled carpenter, it would be the sort of job I would take on just for the beer money.

"I REMEMBER ONE JANUARY NIGHT BEFORE THE PUB WAS IMPROVED, I SIMPLY SLEPT IN MY CLOTHES"

Pushing ever southwards, I crossed over the wild open expanse of Ashdown Forest to Maresfield and checked into the Chequers Inn, where I was domiciled for the next stage of my journey. This quiet, ancient village is really based around a mini-roundabout, at the junction of two B-roads, with an impressive church, the pub and an imposing lodge entrance to Maresfield Park. Evidently Maresfield Park was a military establishment which saw the formation of the 7th Signal regiment in the 1920s, continuing to operate there until 1994. Signal regiments provide combat support, battlefield communication and information systems, which are essential to all effective military operations. The site has since been developed as a residential estate. The village also boasts a convenience shop and post office run by an accommodating Asian gentleman and an extensive recreation ground. I concluded that I would have to sojourn in the Chequers Inn for the remainder of the day and evening, as there was nowhere else to go in this modest village.

On the first morning of this trip, I returned to Lewes by taxi and was dropped off by the eastern pedestrianised section of the High Street. I made my way up to the elegant humpback bridge over the River Ouse and searched for a passage to the left to take me down to the riverbank. Passing through extensive car parks and diving under the ring road, I strode out along a pleasant riverside path to the smell of hops emanating from the Harvey's brewery complex over my left shoulder. I passed alongside a large recreation ground, obviously prone to flooding, before crossing the river at Whalley's Bridge, and picking out the Ouse valley walk on the western side of the substantial river. The day was already hot and threatened to be a real scorcher. Looking across the calm, brown tidal river, I could see a pleasant settlement enclave based around a church, the original settlement of South Malling, now swamped by Lewes. I mused on the fact that I was familiar with places called East and West Malling in Kent but did not know of a North Malling to complete the four major points of the Malling compass.

To my left, across the railway line and the floodplain, was the regimented municipal suburb of Landport, uniformly laid out in a lozenge-shaped pattern, nestling under the last remnants of the South Downs. Further on I could see the distinctive white scar of a disused chalk pit on the side of Offham Hill. Again I was reminded that the nearby village of Offham had its twin in the Kent countryside west of Maidstone. Observing the natural tidal river, it was possible to clearly see the high and low water marks on the opposite riverbank

Map 01: Lewes to Isfield

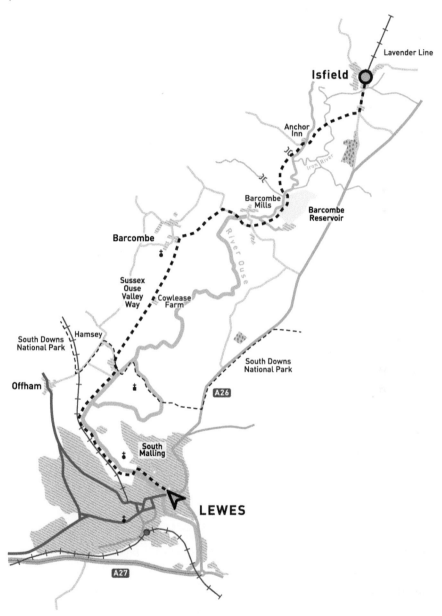

1km

by a strip of muddy dark green salt-affected vegetation. Hiking along beside the river, I was conscious of getting into my stride. Coming out of Lewes I had been stumbling clumsily along but now I could feel the walking rhythm setting in, a satisfying cadence that I knew from experience would eat up the miles.

As the river came close to the busy railway line, it swung violently to the east in an exaggerated loop around a small knoll of fifteen metres, containing the isolated Hamsey Place and Hamsey Place Farm. I kept to the Sussex Ouse Valley Way and carried on beside the back section of the river that cut off the loop with more energetic straightened rushing waters. I noticed that there were many brick-built pillboxes strung out along the valley, a remnant of war defences when invasion up the valley of the River Ouse was considered a distinct possibility. Looking south-east, I could clearly see Malling Hill, part of the dramatic scarp slope of the South Downs, with another large housing estate sprawling out from Lewes below.

At the enticing entrance to the historic Hamsey Place, I left the river and strolled down the lane to the hamlet of Hamsey, which was graced by some charming cottages. I noted that all these properties were located inside the boundary of the recently created South Downs National Park. Here the footpath swung to the right, traversing arable fields to Barcombe village, a distance of a mile and a bit. Some of the fields were full of sweetcorn being harvested and some, having been harvested, were full of stubble waiting to be ploughed in. I crossed the open hedgeless fields which offered no shelter in the baking heat. I trudged on through the back of Crowlease Farm and carried on down to a small stream which I crossed by a wooden footbridge and observed a deep hole in the ground, which housed an active spring surrounded by scruffy unkempt vegetation. It is impossible to underestimate the importance of such places in history and mythology; places where water appeared to magically gush out of the ground, places revered by our ancestors. In that distant past, I have no doubt the spring would have been carefully tended and shown considerable respect, even receiving votive offerings from time to time. Looking at the map, I discerned a number of other springs running to the right forming a spring line, a geological phenomenon, in this case, related to the erosion and retreat of the chalk scarp face of the South Downs. Water percolating through the porous chalk Downs has created a water table coming to the surface at the outer edge of the piedmont, thus creating a spring line. Relying entirely on my memory of studying geomorphology at school, I drew a sketch diagram to explain the phenomenon.

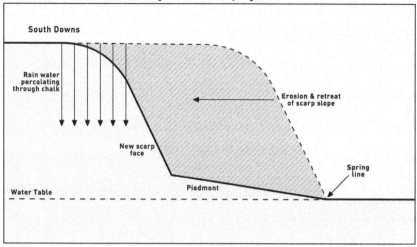

Crossing the seemingly arid fields, I could see the elegant parish church spire of Barcombe village up ahead. Unfortunately, sticking to the footpath, I passed to the east of the village and could only admire the carefully tended grounds of the Court House running down to the footpath. I thought I would visit the village properly one day, and take time to stroll down through its main street when next down this way. Pressing on to a disused railway line, one of a number in this valley, I rested for a while on a style looking back to the South Downs. Dr Beeching's axe seems to have fallen very heavily on this part of East Sussex, creating a network of sinuous empty scars in the landscape. Some disused railway lines have been adapted to be used as footpaths or cycleways, or retained for hobby steam trains, but many more still remain unused and redundant, fossilised in the landscape.

I plodded on to a small lane which led me back to the river in the vicinity of Barcombe Mills. Here, everywhere, there was the sound of water in the air, rushing over many weirs, in the much-divided river. I paused for a while, leaning on an elegant brick-built bridge parapet looking north, trying to make sense of the river, and observed a multitude of small fish shoaling in the fresh water. Looking around, I realised the bridge was the limit of the tidal reach of the River Ouse. My map showed a notation, 'ntl', something I had never seen before, which stands for normal tide limit. To the south, the river was tidal all the way to Newhaven on the coast. To the north, the numerous slack, cleverly manged arms of the river created a rich freshwater habitat graced by a myriad of flying insects, unidentifiable to me. If I was prone to be bitten by insects, I might have been concerned at this buzzing cloud, but luckily, I can't recall having been thus afflicted; an attribute I put down, rightly or wrongly, to my Italian antecedents.

As one would expect from the name 'Barcombe Mills', there were once corn mills in this location dating back to the eleventh century, the original buildings being destroyed by fire in 1939. Further on, the calm pools of the river held back by the weirs were being used as adventurous and unregimented swimming pools by the local noisy kids and excited dogs splashing around. There were also clanking canoes on the river being paddled by children in a mock sea battle, in *Swallows and Amazons* fashion. A dozen or so family groups were picnicking and sunbathing on the riverbank. I got the very strong impression this idyllic location for such recreation was a closely guarded local secret; the inland river resort of Barcombe Mills.

Barcombe parish is an interesting study and typical of such in this area. There are three main centres of population: the old original village, with the parish church which I had skirted; the riverside hamlet of Barcombe Mills, where I now stood, historically taking advantage of commerce generated around the river; and the larger, recently expanded settlement of Barcombe Cross, away from the river. Evidently, as in many other similar examples which I have come across in my travels, villagers were evacuated to Barcombe Cross from the original village in the social reconstruction that took place in England after the ravages of the Black Death. Barcombe Cross, being more accessible to the road network, is now greatly developed, with modern housing estates taking over as the main centre of population in the parish.

I pressed on along the tree shuttered riverbank for a half mile or so, past the large Barcombe reservoir, before crossing over one arm of the river by a footbridge to an island in the stream. Further on, I crossed the main arm of the river by a second footbridge to the western bank and soon I could see the welcoming sight of the Anchor Inn looming up ahead. It was extremely hot and the appealing thought of a couple of pints of beer spurred me on. Back home I researched the origins of the name of this pub, given that I was staying at another pub of the same name later on in this journey, and I discovered it had, enigmatically, something to do with ships and the sea. Maybe once, small ships were able to get this far upriver.

Arriving at the pub, I noted the garden was crammed with lunchtime drinkers soaking up the glorious summer sun, sitting on tables with umbrellas for shade, dotted evenly around on a caged, regimented lawn. Excited dogs and feral children were much in evidence. Eventually I managed to get served with a pint of beer and found a place to perch near to the river by the smelly rubbish bins. Here in this frantically busy pub, there was no chance of engaging in any pleasant banter with bar persons while sitting at the bar, my favourite place. I noticed the pub was really a riverside recreation centre with ice-cream kiosks, entertainment marquis and boats to hire. I assumed the canoes I had seen earlier downstream came from here. Slightly uncomfortable and disappointed with the popular, overcrowded pub, after a single pint, I decided to leave the noise and bustle, cut my losses and press on.

"EVENTUALLY I MANAGED TO GET SERVED WITH A PINT OF BEER AND FOUND A PLACE TO PERCH NEAR THE SMELLY RUBBISH BINS"

I crossed back over the River Ouse by elaborate sluice gates and found the footpath across the flat fields to Isfield, where I was hoping for a proper respite in the pub there. I sat comfortably for a while on a stranded wooden footbridge, dangling my feet over the edge into a dry gulley and consumed a can of cider that I had hidden in my rucksack. The dry stream was an arm of the insignificant Iron River, which rises south of Isfield and wanders aimlessly across the Ouse floodplain. The name, 'Iron River', is a testament to the importance of the Weald's iron industry in the vicinity of Isfield. Sitting there in the shade cast by a large oak tree hard up against the track of another disused railway line, I could hear the merry clatter from the pub across the river drifting over the fields. I was reminded of that passage in the *Gypsy Scholar* by Matthew Arnold when Glanville, sitting in a high field corner above Oxford, could hear 'all the live murmurs of a summer's day'. I think in Glanville's case it was probably more insect-driven than the muted whispers created by the less engaging human species.

I traipsed across more fields, alongside the same dismantled railway, up to a B-road and strolled gratefully into the village of Isfield. I observed the pretty station, still under the obsolete British Railways livery, the terminus of the Lavender Line, a very short hobby line for steam train enthusiasts. Next door to the station was the pub, once appropriately called the Station Hotel, but now called, quite originally, the Laughing Fish. I normally dislike the practice of changing pub names, but in this instance, I was somewhat amused by the new name. I spent a very pleasant lunchtime in the pub, relaxing and drinking the local brew, concocted in the nearby Long Man Brewery, nestling under the South Downs in the Cuckmere Valley in the village of Litlington; a village I had passed through on a previous perambulation. I waited outside the pub before meeting my lift to take me back to the Chequers Inn in Maresfield.

"NEXT DOOR TO THE STATION WAS THE PUB ONCE APPROPRIATELY CALLED THE STATION HOTEL, BUT NOW CALLED QUITE ORIGINALLY THE LAUGHING FISH"

Before turning in, lurking in the bar, I had occasion to engage in a pleasant, if somewhat rambling, drunken afternoon conversation about Brexit, with a local chap slumped in the opposite chair. Needless to say, he shared my own incredulity at the outcome of the recent referendum, deriding the fake news pedalled by the leave campaign. On this journey, talking to various people about the referendum, I had found a different degree of willingness to engage in conversation. Some people, like myself, wanted to share their frustration and exorcise their anger at the result. Others were more sheepish, being slightly embarrassed at the outcome, having voted to leave and not believing that the result would turn out the way it did. Others bombastically celebrated the result, claiming there was a clear mandate to leave; what has become known as the hard Brexit position. This camp is inclined to claim some magical democratic mandate, irritatingly invoking the notion of 'the will of the people' as a justification. This in spite of the fact that there was only a tiny majority in favour of leaving the European Community and that any reasonable interpretation of events would regard the referendum as an opinion poll at one moment in time, and only a justification for exploring the terms of the divorce. Needless to say, I have found it hard to talk to people in this zealous camp.

Next morning, returning to Isfield, I continued walking north, out of the straggly village, towards Ashdown Forest. I started very early to avoid the heat of the day. Passing out of the village, I had occasion to cross the River Uck, which further east gave its name to the large Sussex town of Uckfield. I stood for a while on the bridge and admired the flowing waters; an obligatory habit. The second bifurcated stream was graced by an old mill, which had been converted to residential properties. Researching the village, I determined that the original settlement was much nearer the confluence of the rivers Uck and Ouse, marked by an isolated church and an even older motte and bailey castle. Like many villages, Isfield had migrated towards the now redundant railway away from its historical roots. As I trudged ever northwards, I mused on the fact that so many villages, and towns, in this county had names that end in 'field'. I understand this epithet is equivalent to the 'den' prevalent in south-west Kent remarked on before, meaning essentially the same, a clearing in the forest. The forest, in this case, being the same original wild wood of Anderida which covered the Weald when the Roman legions invaded.

Map 02: Isfield to Maresfield

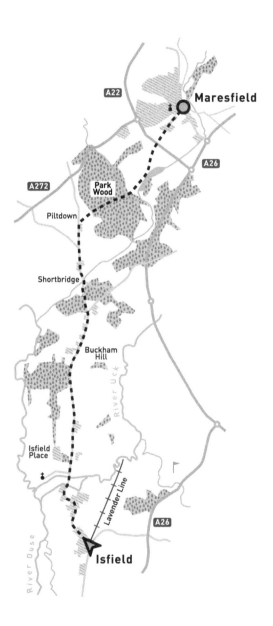

1km

Pressing on up the lane, past an historic but unused animal pound, renovated in 1990 and listed, I wondered if now a useful purpose could be found for this enclosure. As it is, although the structure is intact, the interior is completely overgrown with vegetation and entirely unusable. Such remaining pounds, which are still scattered across south-east England, were used in medieval times to collect up stray livestock which were only released on payment of a fine. Further on, I paused for a while at the entrance to Isfield Place, the local stately pile, and admired the nicely tended lawns running up beside the drive. This Elizabethan manor house, with gardens laid out in the Arts and Crafts style in the late nineteenth century, remained, unlike so many others, still, unfortunately, in private hands. I climbed up the mile-long slope to Buckham Hill at forty-four metres, in the morning rush hour traffic, the highest point on a finger ridge of land between the rivers Ouse and Uck. At the summit, the lane divided, and I took the left-hand fork down, past Pierpoint's Wood, to a small sunken stream at Shortbridge. I passed the appealing Peacock Inn too early in the morning for it to be open, even for coffee.

Further on, the lane forked again and I climbed up to Piltdown golf club close to the Pilt Down, the site of the notorious archaeology hoax. This is where a Mr Charles Dawson, an amateur archaeologist domiciled at the nearby Barkham Manor, claimed to have discovered the missing link between man and apes, the so-called Piltdown Man, doing serious damage to the liberating notion of evolution. I followed the footpath to the right, below Piltdown church, and entered the large open access area that is Park Wood. The dank route through the middle of the wood was clearly articulated on a sunken track that evoked antiquity, no doubt created by the passage of countless feet and hooves over the years. I made good progress along this track and emerged from the trees by a sunny field corner and pressed on beside a large private park with ornamental lakes created by damming the small stream that ran down to Shortbridge Weir. I struggled on along a narrow path fenced tight against a hedgerow festooned with arching head-high brambles scratching my bonce. Next, I skirted Furnacebank Wood with its row of small ponds, further evidence of historic iron making in this vicinity.

Shortly I came up against the traffic-filled A22, the Maresfield bypass, which I crossed with care. Over the road I strolled into the south-western sector of the village, past redundant fields and bright new housing developments. It occurred to me this was a natural place for urban expansion, inside the bypass, where new housing could be combined with amenity open space to create an enjoyable living environment. The redundant field up against the road could be planted up as a wood, to shield the new housing against excessive traffic noise, or used for allotments or other recreation, or even some new housing. Further in along the footpath, there was a wedge of ungrazed land presaging the church that would make a splendid public open space. I just hoped the local authority had a plan to manage the development of this critical south-western quarter of Maresfield, rather than leave it to the unbridled opportunism of housing developers. I felt that if properly handled, the development of this segment could add greatly to the quality of Maresfield as a good place to live. I came up to the impressive church enclosed in a ring of massive lime trees, cleverly, and no doubt laboriously, pruned of their lateral growth to create distinctive majestic straight columns.

Arriving early in Maresfield I decided to drive back over my route to Isfield, but first paid a visit to the pub in Piltdown on the A272, which is now called the Lamb, but used to be called the Piltdown Man. I arrived early and ordered a pint in this free house, typically decked out in the grey and white livery which seems to adorn such enterprises. I tried to engage the barman in discussion about the Piltdown hoax, but he seemed most uninterested. It was as though with the change in the pub's name there was an attempt to exorcise the hoax affair from living memory, or perhaps the staff were just bored with it. The pub seemed to be more interested in promoting itself as a venue for unnecessarily extravagant and expensive weddings rather than a place for discerning drinkers to gather and discuss the significance of evolution and the consequences of this audacious hoax. I can't say, with all honesty, that I blame the proprietors for this change of emphasis and pursuing an undoubtedly more lucrative and sustainable direction.

After a brief stay, I drove through the lanes to Shortbridge, where I had lunch in the Peacock Inn, which I had passed earlier, an unspoilt pub with a pleasant enough atmosphere. After this I drove back south to Isfield, where I checked out the parish church that I had mentioned earlier. It was indeed a very isolated spot down by the River Ouse, accessed by a very narrow and

"I TRIED TO ENGAGE THE BARMAN IN DISCUSSION ABOUT THE PILTDOWN HOAX BUT HE SEEMED MOST DISINTERESTED"

infrequently used lane. The adjacent motte and bailey castle close to the river was overgrown with trees and hardly discernible. I parked up in this quiet spot at the end of the lane, threw back my car seat and had a very satisfying forty winks before driving north to Hartfield. On the way north, though, I had occasion to pop into the Foresters Arms at Fairwarp, just for the sake of seeing what it was like. Fairwarp itself was a pleasant enough village on the southern slopes of Ashdown Forest, with a mixture of houses set off by a narrow village green. I returned to the main road and drove over the exposed forest to my next berth, the Anchor Inn at Hartfield.

In the evening I was joined by my two good old friends from West Malling. After an enjoyable meal, and a few drinks, we were regaled by a trio of musicians in an empty pub. Being curious as to the style of music being played, we were informed that it was 'swing'. The evening's main topic of conversation naturally revolved around the recent narrow preference of the British public to leave the European Union. It was a pleasure to have an intelligent discussion with two people who were equally dismayed as me about the referendum outcome. However, we three agreed that the outcome was not decisive enough to warrant a headlong exit from the Union, but only to explore the terms of the divorce.

Map 03: Maresfield to Hartfield

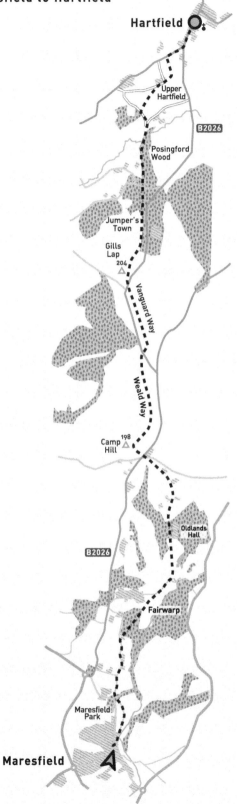

N

Hartfield

Upper Hartfield

B2026

Posingford Wood

Jumper's Town

Gills Lap
204

Vanguard Way

Weald Way

Camp Hill
198

Oldlands Hall

B2026

Fairwarp

Maresfield Park

Maresfield

1km

Next morning, I returned to Maresfield to make an early start, determined to make good progress before the day once again became too hot. Starting again at the Chequers Inn, I walked out of Maresfield after popping into the local shop to buy supplies. I took the lesser Nursery Lane which wound its way ever northwards towards Fairwarp. I progressed above a wooded ravine which naturally limits the possible expansion of the village eastwards. This ravine, carved out by the same small stream mentioned before that runs down to Shortbridge Weir, originates in many tentacles and ponds on the southern slopes of Ashdown Forest, and provided the water power to sustain historic iron making in the vicinity. I plodded along the quiet lane until I hit the inevitable slope, where I was conscious of changing to a lower gear, a more powerful but steady cadence.

Before Fairwarp I peeled off to the right, through the edge of an open access wood, to re-engage with the Wealdway, a major national footpath I had been toying with for many miles. I continued on, climbing all the time through a wooded gulleyed terrain, past elegant dwellings and charming cottages, crunching along on dirt tracks, eventually reaching the stately pile of Oldlands Hall. Further on, a muntjac deer, about the size of a large dog, skipped across the path in front of me. This ancient species of deer, introduced to Woburn Park in Bedfordshire from China, subsequently escaped and is now one of the most common deer in the English countryside since these foreign, secretive animals have no natural predators to keep their numbers in check. Before Crest Farm, the trees which hugged the lower slopes disappeared and I trekked up, above the tree line, to the exposed crossroad junction with the B2026, the Hartfield Road.

I crossed the road and strode up to Camp Hill, at 198 metres, typically marked by a mature clump of scot's pine, one of three native evergreen trees. The definition of native may be disputable, but I take it to be defined by trees which were present on this island at the point in geological time when the land bridge to the continent was severed. The creation of the Channel prevented the further northern spread of tree species chasing the retreat of the ice at the end of the last Ice Age. Incidentally, the other two native species of evergreen trees I understand to be yew and bilberry. Readers might think that holly would qualify, but this species was introduced much later by the Romans. I had occasion to rest a while, in the shade of the trees, sitting on a convenient bench, looking out across the forest slopes to the north-west, taking a well-earned swig from a bottle of water. I made the acquaintance of an elderly dog, who preferred to sit with me than follow her master over the arduous terrain.

After a decent interlude admiring the view, I pressed on along the Wealdway. The next section of the route consisted of a long open sweep across the heart of Ashdown Forest, which epitomised the sparse beauty of this upland. The rutted track on light grey sandy soil up to the main road crossed an open heathland habitat of gorse and heather, the largest of its kind in south-east England. The underlying sandstone rock from the Hastings Beds of the Lower Cretaceous period forms the oldest centre of the heavily eroded Wealden dome. Originally a medieval hunting forest, it was enclosed by twenty-three miles of fencing in 1283 called 'the pale', which was provided with gates to allow commoners access to exercise their grazing rights. The pale literally means a fence made of pales, strips of pointed wood of a light colour, and the forest would have been beyond the pale, a phrase used now to imply something is outside the limits of social convention. I am pleased to say that now walking through the forest can be, by no stretch of the imagination, regarded as anti-social behaviour.

More recently in 1693, large areas of the forest were privatised, leaving only nine-and-a-half square miles as common land. Either side, both east and west of the finger of open access land pointing northwards to Chuck Hatch, one of the original forest gates, there are large, heavily wooded bites taken out of the forest. Coming up to Hartfield Road, I passed a group of cattle huddling together, sheltering from the heat under a solitary misshapen tree. The open heathland was created by commoners using the resources of the forest for grazing, which supressed the growth of trees. The trees were cut down for firewood and used extensively to fuel the iron making industry in both Roman and Tudor times, and bracken, ferns and heather were collected to provide bedding for livestock. Like many commons and lowland heaths in south-east England, modern-day conservation efforts are directed at preventing the inexorable transformation of the landscape back to its climax vegetation, which is forest, thereby protecting the diversity of habitats. As a result, the forest, thankfully, still has a wide variety of iconic flora and fauna, including the skylark and blue gentian. In particular, the conservators are waging a war against the most invasive evergreen shrub, Rhododendron ponticum, which spreads mercilessly unless controlled, by an aggressive suckering root system and abundant seed production.

I reflected on the fact that this wild upland, on the western edge of my patch, is the source of the most significant rivers in south-east England, including the Medway, Rother and Sussex Ouse, the one major exception being the Kentish Stour. I skipped over the busy road and picked up the Vanguard Way, hiking north past the Greenwood Gate clump to my right, the highest point on this part of Ashdown Forest at 223 metres. Hiking along, I mused on the significance of these two long-distance footpaths: the Wealdway (eighty-three miles) and the Vanguard Way (sixty-six miles), both traversing and crossing each other here in the heart of Ashdown Forest. Starting respectively at Gravesend and East Croydon, they both end on the Channel coast nearby to each other in East Sussex, at Eastbourne and Newhaven.

Next I crossed back over the busy B2026 road and climbed up to another distinctive clump of Scots pine at 207 metres. After a short rest and a quick look around, I strolled on to Gill's Lap at 204 metres, the furthest extent of Pooh land. This location is celebrated as the secret place in A. A. Milne's *Winnie the Pooh* stories, which I must confess that I have not read, even to my children. I passed on and tried to strike up a conversation with a fellow walker going my way. Surprisingly he was taciturn and unwilling to converse, so I let him walk on ahead while I dawdled for a while by the memorial to Milne. I strolled on across the sandy heathland by seriously rutted tracks which made walking difficult, taking in splendid views to the north-west across the upper Medway valley, descending gracefully to Jumpers Town and passing back into forested ground on the lower slopes.

I doglegged to the right and came up to a lane leading to Chuck Hatch, which sported a large car park crammed with cars whose decanted occupants were intent on living out a Pooh experience. I walked on down through Posingford Wood and was met by the spectacle of many Pooh devotees picnicking on blankets spread out on the ground in the trees. Mostly I passed parents who were keen to pass on their Pooh obsessions to their bemused children. Then, further on I came to the famous Pooh Sticks Bridge which spanned a fairly insignificant stream which flowed into the River Medway to the east of Hartfield. The bridge was narrow and crowded with people leaning over the parapet to observe the passage of little sticks down the hallowed stream. With a rucksack on my back, I had no option but to unceremoniously barge through, disturbing their concentration on this amazingly futile activity.

"WITH MY RUCKSACK ON MY BACK I HAD NO OPTION BUT TO
UNCEREMONIOUSLY BARGE THROUGH, DISTURBING THEIR
CONCENTRATION ON THIS AMAZINGLY FUTILE ACTIVITY"

Plodding on past Ryecroft Farm, I entered a pleasant enclave of sumptuous dwellings with nicely tended lawns with strident notices forbidding the drooling hoards of Pooh followers to step foot on them. I passed the end of the lane to Cotchford Farm, where A. A. Milne, the author of the Pooh stories, lived, and more importantly, in my view, where my hero Brian Jones of Rolling Stones fame was later drowned in a swimming pool accident in his prime in July 1969, a month after leaving the rock group which he founded. I took the footpath over a steep little ridge across arable fields to Gallipot Hill Farm and came up to the B2110. All that remained now was to stroll down into the accommodating village of Hartfield. At the junction with the road across the forest, the same B2026, I observed a massive oak tree curiously sunk in an artificial round pit and wondered why the hole did not fill with water, thereby compromising the viability of this obviously ancient tree. I strode triumphantly into the village in the early afternoon, determined to repair and enjoy the rest of the day as my labours were complete on this outing.

In the morning I made my way across country to Tenterden, via Tunbridge Wells and the A264 through Goudhurst. After locating the venue of a book fair, I set up stall in the market hall. My hopes of selling any of my books were soon dashed, as it became clear that attendance was limited, given that it was a fine bank holiday weekend, and everybody had gone to the seaside. My prospects were not helped by the very loud and insistent chap next to me, selling his book of fiction, who seemed to frighten off any punters, causing them to avoid my corner of the room. I managed just to break even with the pitch rent and concluded it was a complete waste of a day. I packed up my paraphernalia by mid-afternoon and drove back to Birmingham. I was hopeful that I would be fit enough to carry on walking next year in 2017, starting at Hartfield, completing my foray into East Sussex and passing back into my beloved Kent.

2: Hartfield to Upnor

For the next stage of this epic journey I was based at Southborough, an elegant northern extension of Tunbridge Wells sitting abreast the main A26, the original London to Eastbourne road. Driving down, I stopped off for lunch in the splendid Cock Inn at Ide Hill on the Greensand Ridge. I observed that the pub had been changed round since I last visited, with the bar being located on the other side of the pub. I drove on along the country lanes through Chiddingstone Causeway and Leigh to Hildenborough. Then I passed through the centre of Tonbridge, crossing over the River Medway, and on to Southborough. Here I booked in to the Hand & Sceptre, a well-presented hotel facing on to a splendid, lovingly cared for common, complete with a cricket ground.

In the evening I had a look around the immediate environs, strolling over the common, being amused by a cricket practise organised for very young kids, toddlers really, playing with a soft ball. I thought this was wonderful, being a lovely way to get our young people interested in this superior English game. This pleasing spectacle was only spoiled by the incessant queue of traffic on the A26. I did wonder whether this was endemic or simply a result of the road widening works on the River Hill section of the nearby A21. I remember my father, when talking about his considerable cycling exploits around Kent, as a young man just after the Second World War when such pastimes were extremely popular, identifying River Hill as being the most punishing climb, even worse than Wrotham Hill or Polhill up the North Downs scarp slope. Now this narrow section of the A21, which causes interminable southbound traffic queues, is being widened to link with improved sections of the road around Tunbridge Wells, to provide a fast, new road down into the heart of Kent. I wondered what my dad would think of it if he was still alive.

Returning to Hartfield in the late spring of 2017, I sallied forth, northward, back into Kent, which I had left a few years before, to resume this endless trek. After popping into the local shop for supplies, I walked out down the main street and cut across the corner field, home to retired beef cattle at the junction of two B-roads, the B2026 and B2110. Then I found the footpath through a housing estate, past the Norman motte and bailey castle, now no more than an unregarded, denuded bump in the ground. I slipped down to the disused railway in the upper Medway valley which used to run from East Grinstead to Tunbridge Wells. The easternmost section of this track from Groombridge has now been reclaimed for the Spa Valley railway, another line dedicated to resurrected steam trains. The redundant track north of Hartfield now forms a major part of the route of the Sussex Border Path, much of which elsewhere, in my experience, is much less navigable. On reaching the clearly signposted junction with the Wealdway, after about a quarter of a mile, I turned north to the headwaters of the main river in these parts, the Medway. Although I had toyed with these meandering headwaters before on previous walks, I still stood on the footbridge and marvelled at how small and deeply incised the river was at this point, as it carved its way out of the High Weald. This seventy-mile river has its source at Turners Hill, just west of East Grinstead in East Sussex, and drains a catchment area of 930 square miles and ties the counties of Kent and East Sussex securely together.

I crossed over the river and turned east again, walking along a river cliff situated above the floodplain, all the way to Summerford Farm and beyond. It was difficult walking at times through woods suspended above the flat fields, but there were always splendid views of the fledgling river. Further on, below Hale Court Farm, the Wealdway crossed back over the river, striking north on the right bank. Sitting for a while on an ugly concrete drainage installation, I observed an official-looking Land Rover edging menacingly over field tracks towards me. Being fairly confident that I had not committed any misdemeanour, I stood my ground, or, to be more precise, stayed sitting. The vehicle parked up and disgorged two Environmental Agency workers who politely bid me good morning. I

Map 04: Hartfield to Fordcombe

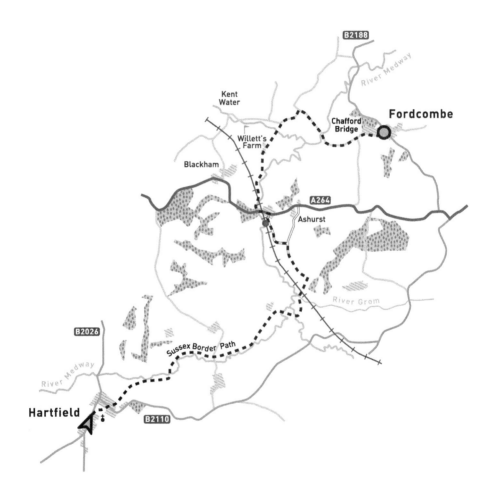

1km

followed these two workers at a respectful distance down to the footbridge over the River Grom, emanating from the lovely village of Groombridge. Here I engaged them in further conversation; they were monitoring water quality in the River Grom before it discharged into the Medway. The River Grom in this vicinity marks the county boundary, a fact that these workers seemed surprisingly unaware of. Overhearing their conversation, it was apparent that one of their number was getting bored with this activity and was hoping to return home to New Zealand.

"ONE OF THEIR NUMBER WAS GETTING BORED WITH THIS ACTIVITY AND WAS HOPING TO RETURN HOME TO NEW ZEALAND"

Passing under an operational railway line this time, I climbed out of the valley and continued with the Sussex Border Path towards Ashurst, up to a height of seventy metres, before dropping down to Jessup's Farm. I came into the nondescript settlement around Ashurst Station, a mile down the road from the village of Ashurst up the hill. Turning west along the main A264, I passed under the railway again and over the river, before picking up the Sussex Border Path on the other side. The path passed back again, with the river, under the railway and hugged the west bank across a widening flat floodplain. Then the walking became difficult and the route hard to follow, an experience, as I have previously mentioned, that is common with this path on the way up to Willett's Farm. I trudged on down to the Kent Water, another significant tributary of the Medway, again like the big river itself, originating in the vicinity of East Grinstead. Climbing up to the next lane, I strolled on down to elegant Chafford Bridge, re-crossing the now more significant river, before slogging up the long, punishing slope into Fordcombe. On this endless climb out of the valley, up to a height of 100 metres, I paused frequently to get my breath.

Gratefully reaching the top of Spring Hill by a small village green, I repaired to the Chafford Arms and spent a pleasant interval sitting in the spacious garden with a few pints, admiring the stunning view across the High Weald. I observed from my map that everything in this vicinity was named Chafford: Chafford Park, Farm and Mill, as well as the bridge and pub. I speculated on the origin of the name, supposing there was some historical figure lurking in the background giving his name to everything on the estate. Subsequently, from my research at home, I was not able to identify such a person, but that doesn't mean that such a person did not exist. Having toiled up the hill into Fordcombe, I decided to call it a day and ordered a taxi to take me back to Southborough.

"I OBSERVED FROM MY MAP THAT EVERYTHING
IN THIS VICINITY WAS NAMED CHAFFORD"

The next day I returned and continued walking east along the Wealdway towards Speldhurst, on through the High Weald. I strode out from Fordcombe along pleasant lanes to Silcocks Farm and beyond, a mile or so of easy level walking. Then, just before Hickman's Farm, on a lane I had walked before, I plunged down into Avery's Wood. I went deeper into the shady wood, along a precarious path, down to a ravine where two small streams joined before flowing out to the Medway through Poundsbridge. Here I made the acquaintance of a friendly labrador running wild ahead of its keepers. As a greeting, the dog decided to shake off the muddy water collected from the stream in an ecstatic quiver from head to tail, and likewise soaked me from head to tail in the process. The apologetic keepers did me the service of directing me up to the nearby lane in Bullingstone, since the way was poorly marked, as some sort of recompense. Once in the lane, the designated path took a short dogleg before issuing out across flat fields on the way to another hilltop village, that is, Speldhurst. This was the second time I had walked through this hilltop village and my impression was very much the same: it lacked a sense of place. I suspect this is due to the fact that it has no clear centre grouped around a village green. I passed on through the grounds of the attractive church, noticing that it was too early for the pub to be open for refreshments, and pressed on towards Southborough.

I dropped down the hill, out of the village, and picked up the Tunbridge Wells Circular Walk, which plunged down into a valley with a derelict watermill. I thought it would be a lovely project to renovate this mill but unfortunately the immediate environs were very shabby, with ugly industrial units detracting from the viability of the enterprise. I crossed over the stream at the bottom and climbed up again to the next lane. Departing from the designated route, I carried on along this high lane to Stockland Green, all the time keeping above 100 metres. Approaching Southborough, plunging into another valley, I crossed the stream that is fed by the nearby Chalybeate Spring. This was the same name as that given to the famous spring in the Pantiles in Tunbridge Wells. Of course, after some research, the reason was made clear, in that 'chalybeate' means iron bearing and thus there are many such springs in the Weald. Then I made the steep ascent to Modest Corner, a curiously named hamlet at the south-west corner of Southborough Common.

Map 05: Fordcombe to Southborough

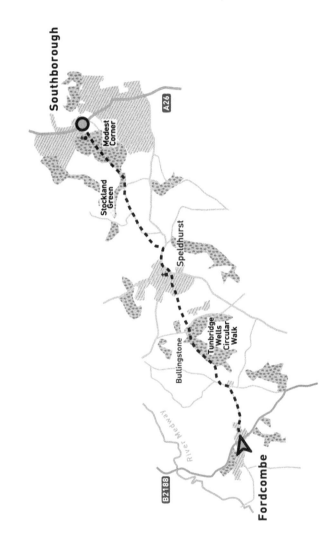

Southborough

Modest Corner

Stockland Green

Speldhurst

Bullingstone

Tunbridge Wells Circular Walk

River Medway

A26

B2188

Fordcombe

1km

Sauntering on across the common, along the Tunbridge Wells Circular Walk, through a lovely naturally wooded open access area of seventy-one acres in extent, I came right up to Southborough church. I exploded onto the manicured part of the common in triumph and sat for a while on a seat designed to look over the cricket ground, luxuriating in the realisation that the day's labours were over. A delicious moment indeed that made the trek over the High Weald from Fordcombe worth every step. I rested for a while before crossing back over the busy A26 to locate my car in the Hand and Sceptre car park. I then drove on to my next berth, in the Rose and Crown in Tonbridge, a historic hotel right in the centre of the town that I had stayed in before. Out and about in the evening, I returned again to the Man of Kent pub just north of the river for an evening of enjoyable quizzing. The name of the pub is itself a curiosity, since men born north of the River Medway, like me, are known as Kentish men, not Men of Kent. However, never mind, in the singular, it is still a splendid name for a pub. Having stayed in Tunbridge a number of times in my rambles around the county, I have always found it to be an agreeable experience.

After returning to Southborough by taxi in the morning, I strolled out across the common towards Bidborough. I passed behind the backs of pleasant dwellings, noting local indignation about a proposed housing development on adjacent fields. I have to agree with the residents here that the proposed development on this high land at 125 metres would totally obliterate the fabulous view of the present incumbents, and walkers using the footpath, out across the High Weald. I read the statutory planning notice and the more frequently posted local objections pinned to every available wooden post. I concurred with the argument of the objecting residents that any development would add to the intolerable traffic congestion on the A26 in this vicinity. I slid down into a cherished valley and clambered back up, past the village school, to the hilltop village of Bidborough. It was a steep, lung-splitting climb up to the church perched precariously on the summit at over 100 metres in the centre of the old village.

Leaving the Wealdway, I trekked northwards out to the main road, the B2176, through the newer expansion of the village. I crossed over the main road by the new village centre and took the quiet lane opposite, leading

Map 06: Southborough to Hildenborough

N

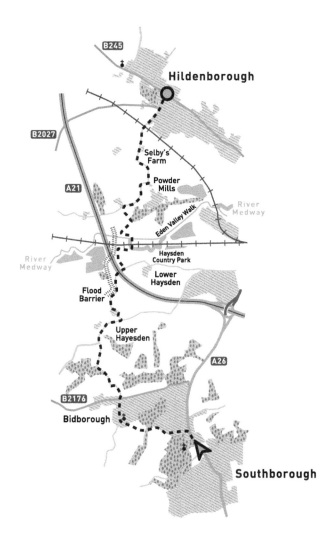

B245

Hildenborough

B2027

Selby's
Farm

A21

Powder
Mills

Eden Valley Walk

River
Medway

Haysden
Country Park

River
Medway

Lower
Haysden

Flood
Barrier

Upper
Hayesden

A26

B2176

Bidborough

Southborough

1km

down out of the Weald. It was a pleasant walk meandering ever northwards. I did, however, have to negotiate a difficult traffic-strewn stretch of the B-road past Upper Hayesden before gratefully turning down the lane that catches the tail of the flood barrier. The barrier consists of a carefully mown mound that snakes it way across the Medway valley, connecting contours at twenty-five metres on both sides of the valley. The so-called Leigh flood storage area was built in 1982 to reduce the risk of flooding in Tonbridge and other communities downstream. It has a capacity of over 5.5 million cubic metres of water and is the largest flood catchment area of its kind in the UK. The gentle lane passed underneath the A21 and I took a bridleway alongside the thunderous road in the sky to the straight mile. Here the barrier also insinuated itself underneath the trunk road and I clambered up the bank and sat for a while, looking down into the now dry reservoir bowl filled with luxuriant vegetation.

I turned back towards Tonbridge along the eastern section of the straight mile, which is now cut in two by Haysden Water, before striking north again. I squeezed under a railway tunnel, dripping with water, hard up against a slack backwater of the main river. I carried on, crossing the Medway by a footbridge, a route I had taken before, passing the other way. Then, turning west, I strolled back to the flood barrier on the other side of the river and stood for a while, stunned by the massive river gates designed to hold back the stream in times of flood. Picking up a footpath, which went off at an acute angle across a field of ripening wheat, I made my way across the extensive floodplain. Finally, crossing another backwater of the big river, I climbed out of the valley to the next brown lane, the twisting lane from Leigh to Hildenborough.

Reaching the lane, I turned east, bypassing the redundant Powder Mills. The Leigh Powder Mills at Ramhurst, just to the west of Tonbridge, were employed from 1813 to 1934 in the making of that all-important historic commodity, namely gunpowder. Water from the Medway was used to turn water wheels providing the power to grind the gunpowder, and the river provided the means to transport the finished product downstream to the River Thames. The works, which have been redundant since their closure, is now being developed for new, expensive housing. I popped into the local pub, The Plough, a traditional country pub, which would have served the workers from the Powder Mills when they were active. Now a little off the beaten track, I imagine the proprietors will be delighted at the prospect of custom emanating from the nearby housing development. After a short rest, I pressed on to Hildenborough. By a gradually ascending road I made my way past Selby's Farm and under the railway line, and slogged up a final rise through mundane housing estates. The end of this particular leg of my journey ended in the Flying Dutchman in Hildenborough, on the B245, an unprepossessing pub given over to the broadcasting of sport.

From Hildenborough I decided to catch a bus back into Tonbridge, but together with an increasingly impatient and restless crowd, I waited for what seemed like ages for the bus to arrive. The locals philosophically explained that the buses around here were very unreliable and rarely kept to the times stated on the bus timetable. While I waited for the bus, I remembered that years ago on another walk, when painfully struggling along this stretch into Tonbridge, my right knee had blown up like a balloon. In the evening, sojourned in the Rose and Crown hotel, I applied lashings of painkilling gel to my knee to assuage the pain and next morning I manged to carry on. However, I guess with the painkillers still in my system masking the pain, the damage done by further walking contributed to my need to have an operation in the future to clean out the offending joint.

I returned to Tonbridge, picked up my car and drove on to my next venue, that is, Royal Tunbridge Wells. I checked into the splendour of the Swan Hotel, now renamed as the Tunbridge Wells hotel, after parking up across the road on the common. The back of the hotel faces prosaically onto the common whilst the front forms an integral part of the famous Pantiles. In the evening, after treating myself to a sirloin steak in the hotel, I mooched around the elegant Pantiles. Later, sitting outside the hotel with a long gin and tonic, the heavens opened, but, being situated under a large umbrella canopy, I was able to eccentrically stay outside and enjoy the spectacle of the downpour, as everyone else scampered for cover. The next day I was to try another book fair, in an effort to sell some of my admittedly excellent books, unfortunately with little success. Setting up in a nearby community hall, I started to write up this adventure to counteract the boredom. I did, however, persuade the organiser of the book fair, employed by the nearby Harrington's Rare Book Shop, to take ten of my books to sell in the shop. By mid-afternoon I had had enough, so I packed up my paraphernalia and drove back home to Birmingham, already planning the next leg of my journey.

I returned to Tunbridge Wells again later in the summer to deliver these books to Harrington's and resume my journey. After dropping off my books, I relaxed with a pint, sitting outside the Duke of York in the Pantiles. The ambiance of the multi-levelled spaces was very pleasing, and the beer fine, but the tables being unstable on the cobbled surface were irritating. After this pleasant interlude, I drove north again, via Shipbourne and Ightham, to The Bull Hotel in the classic village of Wrotham, nestling under the North Downs. I had stayed in the Bull a number of times before and was impressed once again by the antiquity of this former coaching inn on the A20, the London to Folkestone road. I spent the early evening sitting at the bar, waiting for food to be served, and got talking to a Purple Bricks salesman. He reported on his burgeoning success as an estate agent, travelling all over the country, working for an outfit that had cornered the modern internet market. The effect that this conversation about the ruthless process of selling houses was to have on me was to remind me of the tyranny of the free market mechanism and the evils of capitalism; not, I think, what he had intended. Later, I had a stroll around the village and popped into the other two pubs – the Rose & Crown, and George and Dragon – before returning to the Bull for a nightcap. I was surprised to see that the Purple Bricks man was still holding forth at the bar, making even less sense than earlier when he was relatively sober.

On the Tuesday morning, I caught a taxi back to the Flying Dutchman in Hildenborough to resume my escapade. I called into a chemist to buy bottled water before proceeding up Cold Harbour Lane. I strolled out northwards past pleasant dwellings down to the Hilden Brook, a stream that joins the Medway in Tonbridge. I carried on down the quiet lane past Trench Farm to the isolated hamlet of Coldharbour and beyond, until the lane petered out in the agreeable morning sunshine. I observed a massive toadstool, as big as a dinner plate, by the side of the track, which seemed to demand to be picked. I managed, with some effort, to resist its sinister intentions. Rising all the time, I passed through Tinley Lodge Farm and noticed that all the land hereabouts belonged to the Fairlawne Estate, whose proprietors insisted on posting intimidating 'keep out' notices everywhere. I couldn't help thinking they were slightly obsessive in protecting their privacy. I passed through Peacock Wood, and by the paddocks of West Green Farm came up to the Hildenborough road.

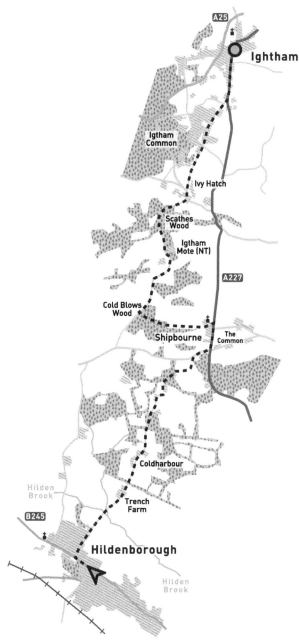

N

A25

Ightham

Igtham
Common

Ivy Hatch

Scathes
Wood

Igtham
Mote (NT)

A227

Cold Blows
Wood

Shipbourne

The
Common

Coldharbour

Hilden
Brook

B245

Trench
Farm

Hildenborough

Hilden
Brook

1km

I elected to walk out to the main A227 because I wished again to pass through the centre of the attractive village of Shipbourne, which I understand is pronounced 'Shibbun' by locals. After a stiff climb up to the village along the busy road, I rested for a while outside the Chaser Inn, splendidly situated opposite the sumptuous common, thankfully now designated as an open access area. After a pleasant interlude observing the scene, I passed out through the churchyard searching for a footpath, the Greensand Way no less, across country to Ightham Mote. At the back of the churchyard, I was faced by the prospect of a massive open ploughed field, across which there was little chance of picking up any footpath. I stood for a while and surveyed the way ahead. The absence of any signposts or evidence of a footpath across this field didn't seem right. Uneasily, I set my sights on a wooded field corner in the distance and struck out across the rutted soil. I got the very strange sensation that the tractor ploughing across the other side of the field was keeping a close eye on me. Later I was to discover that in 2011 this footpath, the Greensand Way from the back of St Giles church, was the subject of a dispute, with locals protesting at plans by the landowners, the Fairlawne Estate, to close it. I felt my rambling antennae had picked up this atmosphere, thus accounting for my unease.

Reaching the wooded corner, I realised I had arrived at Cold Blows Wood and that I had lost the Greensand Way further to the north. If I had followed the unmarked route of the Greensand Way, I would have passed close to the tractor ploughing. At the corner of the wood, I got talking to a chap out walking his dog, describing, with some modesty, my exploits. He was genuinely interested, being an energetic outdoor type himself, and I was able to furnish him with a flyer about my books, which I just happened to have on my person. He promised me he would look me up on my website when he got home. I pressed on through the shady wood to Mote Lane.

Thus, after this short detour, I turned north and slogged up the lane towards the Greensand scarp slope. I pressed on to the incredibly impressive and beautifully restored National Trust property of Ightham Mote. Much has been said about this splendid medieval manor house nestling in a south-facing valley cutting though the Greensand Ridge. Indeed, I had passed through here on a previous walk and visited the property and grounds myself on a number of occasions. As I walked northwards alongside the manor house, I was surprised at how far the estate stretched back into the hillside. The small stream running down the valley is sufficient to feed a number of ornamental lakes gracing the extensive landscaped grounds.

Approaching Scathes Wood, there was a lung-splitting, never-ending climb up to 159 metres at the hilltop village of Ivy Hatch on top of the Greensand Ridge. I paused on a number of occasions to get my breath, even resorting to that well-practised routine of counting fifty painful steps before allowing myself a rest. Exhausted by the climb, I retired to the Plough Inn at the top of the hill for respite and lunch. I sat outside the front of the pub on a terrace, enjoying the rest, luxuriating with the sun on my back, drying off my sweat-laden clothes. I remember thinking that there was nothing better than this sensation, maybe even better than sex. I decided to end the day's labours at this point and ordered a taxi to take me back to Wrotham.

"THERE WAS NOTHING BETTER THAN
THIS SENSATION – MAYBE BETTER THAN SEX"

During the taxi ride I got talking to the driver about my observations of the Fairlawne Estate. The driver was a mine of information and informed me that this massive 1,000-acre estate stretching from Shipbourne to Plaxtol was owned by a Saudi Arabian horse breeding prince, one of the richest men in the world. Evidently he rarely visited, but I mused on the fact that his henchmen had manged to upset the locals over the attempted closure of the Greensand Way from the back of Shipbourne church. In the evening I was joined by my friends and we had a meal in the Bull before sampling the other two pubs in Wrotham that I had visited the previous evening. My friend let slip that he very traditionally and properly proposed to his wife many years ago in the Rose & Crown. I admitted that I had not done anything of that conventional sort with my ex-wife, now deceased, but it formed an interesting topic of conversation with the pub landlord. I did think that this revelation at least deserved a free pint but unfortunately nothing was forthcoming.

In the morning, I resumed my journey from the Plough Inn at Ivy Hatch. Again, during the taxi ride, a different driver recounted all the famous people living hereabouts, including Len Goodman of *Strictly Come Dancing* fame, who evidently lived in the historic heart of Ightham. He also suggested to me that in spite of the little spat with our Arabian prince over the footpath issue, locals were in fact very much on his side, since evidently he had paid for a new £50 million gas pipeline from Farningham to Hadlow, thereby ensuring gas supplies to local farms and houses; indeed, supplying gas to much of south-east England. I headed off along a narrow undulating lane beset with comfortable dwellings set in large grounds on the dip slope of Greensand Ridge.

I was keen to make good progress, as the weather was due to turn inclement at about lunchtime. I had debated with myself whether to come down into Ightham from the west via the village of Oldbury but chose instead to carry straight on to join the busy A227. As a consequence, I had to negotiate a perilous stretch of Bates Hill down to the village of Ightham. A number of times I had to jump onto the narrow verge, hard up against hedges to avoid oncoming traffic. I even resorted to crossing over to the wrong side of the main road to give the speeding traffic coming up the hill the opportunity to see me on blind left-hand bends. If any reader is tempted to follow my route I would thoroughly recommend, if one has the time, of taking the Oldbury option. Although the A25, which originally ran through Ightham, is now bypassed, the surprisingly busy A227 still thunders through negotiating a bottleneck caused by the closely situated historic buildings in the centre of the village. I wondered whether a second bypass to the east, taking north/south traffic on the A227 out of the village would be practicable, thereby completely relieving this historic village of through traffic.

I reluctantly passed by the handsome George & Dragon Inn, negotiated my passage through the bottleneck in the heart of the village managed by traffic lights and strode on out of the village, up the long, straight Fen Pond Road. I tunnelled under the A25 and crossed over the adjacent railway line, probing ever northwards. I had been warned by my taxi driver to look out for speeding vehicles along this long, straight stretch too and again I was forever hopping on and off the grass verge. Next I passed through the concrete roots of the M25 and shuffled on, along the Exedown Road, towards the North Downs scarp slope looming large in the distance.

Gradually, rising all the time, I walked onto the heavily ploughed open fields of the distinctive chalk piedmont. I have described this geomorphological feature earlier in this narrative in relation to the South Downs, north of Lewes, created by the erosion and gradual retreat of the scarp slope of the North Downs in this case. I came up to the crossroads with the Kemsing road, crossing a route previously taken, and carried on to the Pilgrims' Way. It was almost as if this lane was crossing the grain of the land with all the communications going east/west in this corridor in the vale below the North Downs. Looking east towards Wrotham, I could clearly see Blacksole Field, the site of the battle of Wrotham Heath leading to the defeat of the rebel Sir Thomas Wyatt of Allington Castle near Maidstone at the hands of Bloody Mary in 1554. Wyatt and his followers objected to the marriage of the monarch to a Catholic Spanish prince and after the collapse of the rebellion, the ensuing backlash against protestants resulted in the death of around seventy people in Kent, the last of whom was John Corneford, a Wrotham man, in 1558.

When I reached the hairpin bend at the base of White Hill on Exedown Road, I found a bridleway which traversed the steep slope of the chalk scarp of the North Downs. This stiff climb would take me up to and across the M20 motorway at the top of Wrotham Hill. The entrance to the bridleway was overgrown and impassable, and I was forced to return to the road and take a parallel track littered with discarded massive tractor tyres. I picked up the bridleway further on and continued my belay across the slope. I could not help but notice the damage done to the path by opportunist mountain bike activity. The speeding bikes had

N

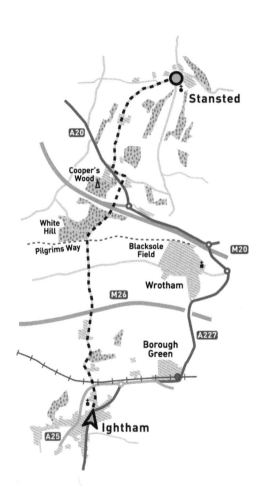

Stansted

A20

Cooper's
Wood

White
Hill

Pilgrims Way

Blacksole
Field

M20

Wrotham

M26

A227

Borough
Green

A25

Ightham

1km

succeeded in releasing quantities of flint nodules from their chalky confinement, making the path uneven and difficult to negotiate. I wondered if the bikers were conscious of the damage they were doing to the footpath in pursuit of the thrills associated with careering down the slope at speed on two wheels.

I emerged on top of the North Downs by a pedestrian bridge over the M20 magnificently raking the sky. I paused for a while in the middle of the bridge and gazed down on the speeding traffic below, a route I had driven along countless times. I remembered years ago, travelling back from the coast with my then-wife in her blue Mini Cooper, before I was able to drive. The car overheated struggling up the long slope and broke down at the top of the hill underneath my feet. I trudged on through noisy fields under the distinctive radio mast in Coopers Wood to the A20, the original trunk road. I skipped over the thoroughfare to the curiously named Labour-in-Vain road. Researching the origins of the name of this road, I could only find one other example, and that was in America; that is, the historic House on Labor-in-Vain road in Ipswich, Massachusetts, New England, built in 1720. I can't imagine there is any relevant connection, particularly as they've spelt 'Labour' incorrectly, but I found no explanation for the road's name. Following the road round a right-angled bend, past a long-forsaken pub, I sauntered on along a high lane to the village of Stansted.

Walking on, I observed a burgeoning dry valley, originating high up on the Downs, close to the scarp slope edge, which swept all the way down to Stansted. I was conscious of marked change in the scenery; the soft rounded contours of the chalk landscape evoked a sense of peace and quiet. It was a pleasurable stroll down the lane into the village buried deep in the contours of the dry valley. I realised this was the first time I had encountered the seductive curves of the chalk landscape since I had left the South Downs last year. This sinuous valley, like many others on the chalk downs, was thought to have been created by meltwater from the retreating ice sheet at the end of the last Ice Age. I carried on down Plaxdale Green Road to a low point, where the dry valley crossed over, before climbing back up a short rise to the village of Stansted. I plodded up to the church, in a hidden secretive village, before retiring to the Black Horse public house at exactly midday.

I spent an awkward lunchtime in this pub assailed by the ceaseless cacophony created by groups of women with their ample broods. I had tried on a number of occasions to book accommodation in this pub but had been rejected on the phone by the rather intimidating landlady. It would appear that all the accommodation had been taken by people attending race meetings at the nearby Brands Hatch circuit. This lunchtime, she kept regarding me with a suspicious gaze while I was eating food at the bar. There was an unfortunate ambiance for me, created by horrible music perpetuated by dodgy crooners, just the sort of music my dad liked. However, the several pints of Larkins ale were agreeable. I concluded, in spite of effusive recommendations by a local taxi driver, that this was not my type of pub. At one o'clock precisely, the promised rain materialised with a vengeance, effectively washing out the afternoon, so I ordered a taxi to take me back to Wrotham. Here I picked up my car and drove on to my next venue at the historic Leather Bottle pub in Cobham.

After a decent afternoon rest, I sat out the evening in this commodious pub, resisting the temptation to stroll down the High Street to sample the other two pubs in the well-preserved village, due to incessant summer rain. This pub was a favourite drinking place of Charles Dickens, who lived for a while at nearby Gadshill up the hill from Rochester on the road to Gravesend. Evidently he used to hike out to Cobham, a round trip of about seven miles, no doubt seeking inspiration for his lugubrious and moralistic novels. To celebrate the fact of his patronage, the walls of the pub are festooned with Dickens memorabilia. There was even a large, recognisable picture of the great man in pride of place behind the bar. I wonder what his favourite tipple was. Somehow I can't quite see him quaffing pints of ale.

"SOMEHOW I CAN'T QUITE SEE HIM QUAFFING PINTS OF ALE"

In the morning, feeling a bit worse for wear, I caught a taxi back to Stansted. The weather was promised to be fine with the odd shower. When I arrived at The Black Horse in Stansted, I found that odd but rather heavy shower reinforcing my gloomy impression of the place from yesterday. I trekked out of the village, down the lane, past the war memorial and found the footpath out of the valley. I sheltered for a while under some trees opposite the solid memorial, trying not to get too wet. This striking edifice consists of a nude male figure looking straight ahead, holding a palm branch in outstretched arms set on a tall square pedestal. This sculpture by Faith Winter is a recent installation; the original statue, by the Hungarian sculpter Alois Stroebl, was stolen in 1995, presumably to be melted down as scrap. Climbing steeply out of the valley and looking back down onto the village, the brief shower having cleared, it was possible to observe its full extent. It lies almost hidden, spider-like, in a multi-headed dry valley which leads eventually down to Longfield.

I followed a high footpath across the chalk downs to Hodsoll Street, an invigorating walk of about a mile. I reflected on the prevalence of place names in this vicinity called something 'street', including Sole Street and Gold Street. I'm not entirely sure why this is, except that I have observed that these settlements do not generally contain a parish church. I tramped on through the twists and turns of Hodsoll Street, noting the presence of a large holiday park, and picked up Rosemary Lane, which propelled me ever northwards towards Meopham Green. At a sharp bend in the lane before the hamlet of New Street, I took a bridleway named as Ifield Road. At this point I thought I should try a bit of yodelling but to be Frank I think I may not have done that famous singer justice. This path descended into another steep gulley, a deep dry valley that stretches down to Luddesdown and Cuxton on the River Medway, which I had previously explored and commented on.

Further on, and not for the first time on this perambulation, I came up to the surprisingly busy and narrow A227, and strolled into Meopham Green past what seemed to me to be a half-hearted nursery enterprise. The traffic on the road, which I seemed to have been toying with for many days, was incessant at this point, just as at Shipbourne and Ightham. This local distributor gives access to the surprisingly large settlements of Culverstone Green and the Vigo village high up on the North Downs, the settlement south of Meopham station and Istead Rise to the north, leading

Map 09: Stansted to Cobham

N

Cobham

Sole Street

B260

Camer Park

Meopham

Mill

Meopham
Green

New Street

Hodsoll
Street

Culverstone
Green

A227

Stansted

1km

"... A DEEP DRY VALLEY THAT STRETCHES DOWN TO LUDDESDOWN AND CUXTON WHICH I HAD PREVIOUSLY COMMENTED ON"

to Gravesend. These greatly expanded, primarily commuter villages, consist of new settlements that have skipped through the confines of the green belt that surrounds London in an attempt to limit its outward growth. The presence of all these settlements testify only to the partial success of this much-cherished planning policy.

Meopham Green is an attractive spot, set as it is around a triangular green, an historic cricket venue with a pub appropriately called the Cricketers. I had often thought that it would be a good project to catalogue all the pubs in Kent and Sussex with a reference to cricket, and maybe even sample all those still remaining. Pubs named Bat and Ball, and other references to the great summer game would also qualify. Meopham Green also has a large, broody windmill with extravagant white sails to catch the wind, lurking behind the pub away from the road. Slogging ever northwards, past a large school and up to the parish church, I discerned that there is little else of merit in the village of Meopham proper. I located a footpath from the back of the churchyard which issued out by a curious little tunnel under a private drive to Meopham Court, the local big house, into the countryside.

I trekked on in good spirits along well-marked footpaths by field edges through extensive swathes of ripening corn. I crossed over Camer Park Road and clipped the corner of Henley Wood, crossed over the Wealdway again, strolled on under power lines, to come up against the railway. Crossing the railway by a surface walkway, I disgorged into a well-kept apple orchard with a clearly marked footpath going diagonally across lines of fruit trees on dwarfing rootstock. Later in this massive plantation, walking alongside a windbreak of pollarded trees designed to protect the precious crop, I did lose the way. I came to an east/west footpath and, working out where I was on the map with the aid of a double row of overhead power lines, I turned east up the slope in this dessert apple desert towards Cobham.

I came into the much-anticipated village by the back door, by the earnestly religious Cobham College, attached to the main impressive church famous for its brass rubbings. I had a quick poke around but could see no evidence of active religious indoctrination and passed on through the churchyard to The Street. As it was early, I decided to pop into the Darnley Arms, where I bumped into the assistant manager of the Leather Bottle, who was practising his darts. Lord Darnley, whom the pub was named after, was a significant historical figure in the Tudor court, a favourite of Queen Elizabeth I, and the owner of nearby Cobham Hall. A later Lord Darnley was a key player in the 'Ashes affair' and the creation of the diminutive cricket trophy ardently fought over by England and Australia for many years since. After a couple of pints, I returned to my berth in the Leather Bottle for rest and recuperation.

In the evening I was joined by my same two friends I met in Wrotham, who have followed my perambulations through Kent with interest and encouragement. We indulged in a pub crawl up The Street, first visiting the Ship Inn at the far end and then the Darnley Arms before returning to the Leather Bottle. The presence of three seemingly viable pubs in such a small village is no doubt due to the patronage of people living in the nearby major Kentish town of Gravesend. My friends were thrown out at closing time but being a guest, I was allowed to prop up the bar for some time after.

On the next morning, a Friday, I set out again down the narrow and elegant traffic calmed street towards Cobham Park. At the roundabout, at the end of The Street, by the war memorial, where the ceremonial avenue leads on to Cobham Hall, I took the bridleway that is Lodge Lane. I strolled

Map 10: Cobham to Upnor

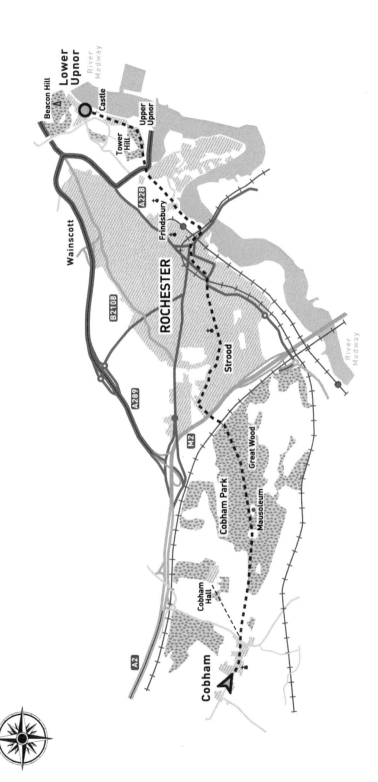

along the lane, well past Lodge Farm, in the uplifting morning sunshine to reach a large wooded area in National Trust care known as Cobham Woods. These impressive woods were evidently, according to a helpful information board, one of the best examples of how lowland Britain would have looked in historical times. The open woods were populated with gnarled mature oak trees and sweet chestnuts with their deeply scarred spiralling bark pattern, with an understorey of ferns and brambles. The woods were delightfully grazed by highland cattle, whose purpose, apart from being good to look at, was to keep the habitat open, light and authentic. I came across a group of three of these cattle grazing by the track with a magnificent bull only reluctantly moving out of the way to let me pass. There were many dead, bleached-white trees naturally left standing and fallen trees – casualties of the 1987 storm left prone on the ground to sport, in some cases, amazing new vertical secondary growth. This was an invigorating walk through a natural and what I hesitate to say is an 'unmanaged' wood, which I would highly recommend.

"I CAME UPON A GROUP OF THREE OF THESE CATTLE GRAZING BY THE TRACK WITH A MAGNIFICENT BULL ONLY RELUCTANTLY MOVING OUT OF THE WAY TO LET ME PASS"

In the centre of the wood, along the ridge that I was following, at a place known as William's Hill, was the Darnley Mausoleum, an imposing stone building of mammoth but tasteful proportions. This Grade I listed building was restored and is owned by the National Trust; it sits on the highest point of the former Cobham Hall estate. It was built to house the remains of the 4th Earl Darnley and his descendants when the family plot in Westminster Abbey was full but was never actually used for this purpose because the building was never consecrated. This iconic building now stands like a folly in the centre of the National Trust estate of Cobham Woods. I'm not sure what practical use the building is put to now. The incredibly satisfying landscape continued into the Great Wood of Ranscombe Farm Park but here there was more evidence of former woodland management in the guise of coppicing. The path through the woods descended gently off the ridge to the railway, the HS1 line to St Pancras station no less, which I crossed by an iron pedestrian bridge. Next, I plunged under the motorway by a heavily graffitied tunnel, strewn with dubious litter suggesting certain unsavoury activities, to disgorge into Strood, the north-western manifestation of the urban area of the Medway Towns.

This suburb of the Medway Towns, which is disported on a hillside above the River Medway at Rochester, is dominated by vast council estates. As I walked down the hill I observed, as an alien sociologist might, the life of the inhabitants, dominated by buses, clapped-out vans, mobile phones and rubbish bins. Although the municipal grass verges were neatly trimmed and the burnt-out vehicles assiduously removed, the places where they were incinerated were identified only by a burnt patch on the ground. There seemed to be an active community spirit here, with people actually conversing with each other by the shops and in doorways. Towards the bottom of the long slope the houses became older, and no doubt less desirable, some being given a much-needed overhaul by the local authority, with their contents being unceremoniously dumped by the roadside waiting for collection.

At the bottom of the hill I passed under the railway line and was immediately greeted by the traffic-dominated mayhem that is Strood town centre. Here is a combination of fast, busy roads, worn-out retail and industrial premises, and new sparkling offices and shopping malls, gathering up on the west bank to spill across the Medway bridge to join with the rest of the Medway Towns. I found my way past the civic centre to the north-west side of the 'new' south-east bound Medway Bridge constructed in 1969. On this occasion the bridge was not undergoing major repair, but like the proverbial Forth Road Bridge, it was only being painted. I picked up the Saxon Shore Way by the river and strode out of Strood along a waterfront dominated by buddleia-haunted derelict wharfs. Looking back across the river, I paused a number of times to admire the prospect of historic Rochester piled up around and dominated by its impressive castle. Further on in Frindsbury, I reached the place where the Gravesend and Rochester canal once entered the Medway. The now-disused seven-mile long canal, cutting across the Hoo Peninsula from Gravesend, used to run through the lengthy Higham tunnel, now occupied by the railway, and formed a short cut for barges from the River Thames to the Medway.

Ahead I could see the sheer white chalk face of the quarry prefacing the ancient doomsday settlement of Frindsbury, now swamped in the urban sprawl, with its church teetering on the edge of the man-made cliff. I climbed up the down by a narrow footpath on a precarious strip of unquarried ground which fell away steeply on both sides. I passed by the parish church to my left, missing the historic centre, and proceeded down along a scruffy deserted road, observing a chap sleeping in his car with his legs sticking out of the car window. I concluded that this backwater was only suitable for nefarious purposes and I hurried on to a busy bright new roundabout giving access to the very useful Medway Tunnel.

I crossed the tunnel approach road by a pedestrian crossing. When the lights suddenly changed, as they have a habit of doing, a heavy oncoming juggernaut slammed on its hissing brakes, having great difficulty in stopping in time. I waved to the stressed but relieved driver in thankful acknowledgement of his herculean efforts to bring the massive lorry to a juddering halt, but I think he was less than impressed. I carried on along a footpath alongside the tunnel approach, nearly being mown down by a cyclist from behind. Then I negotiated a narrow, overgrown section of footpath hard up against a chain-link fence guarding a slightly intimidating Ministry of Defence riverside establishment, with the appropriate plethora of 'KEEP OUT' notices, around the base of Tower Hill. I wondered what useful defensive activities were promulgated from this marine location, or whether the military staff were just having fun playing about in boats.

I emerged joyfully onto a spirit-uplifting sandy footpath along the river's margin at Upnor Reach. Here there was a strip of occasionally submerged dry land sporting low-growing salt tolerant vegetation which would only be inundated at the highest tides. I paused for a while in my headlong rush and sat on a concrete wall at the back of the strand, which was designed to contain the waters in times of flood, and observed the scene. I looked out across the river toward Chatham with many fragile yachts dotted about on the surface of the wide estuary. Peace flooded down on me, sitting there in the sunshine, with dragonflies flitting around my head. I pinpointed the site of the old Chatham Docks across the river to my right where Royal Navy ships were scuppered and towed away by the marauding Dutch in 1667 in the so-called battle of the Medway. It seems strange now to accept that the Dutch were once mortal enemies, since now we seem to get on okay. But then we were at war at a time when both countries were gobbling up parts of the globe in the lucrative promotion of empire. This was the third calamity to strike England in the troubled reign of Charles II after the Great Plague of 1665 and the Great Fire of London in 1666.

All that remained now was to stroll up to Upnor with its attractive assemblage of riverside properties. I poked my head through the open gates of Upnor Castle, managed by English Heritage, ineffective to guard against the aforesaid raid. Triumphantly I walked up the narrow, cobbled street, lined with quaint cottages and repaired to the much-recommended Kings Arms on the corner, the end of this leg of my marathon journey. I sojourned at the bar with crayfish sandwiches washed down with a few pints of real ale. Looking round the pub, I could see that the walls were festooned with meritorious plaques celebrating the quality of the beer and cider sold in the pub over recent years. I explained to the bar staff that I had long wished to sit there at the bar of this pub and sample its beer because it had been highly recommended to me by my barber in Kings Heath Birmingham, who grew up in the Medway towns. The landlord appeared to be vaguely amused by this revelation, but when I next had a haircut back home, my barber was more enthused. After a decent rest, I took the last dregs of my third pint outside and waited for a taxi to take me back to Cobham. I spent another convivial evening in the Leather Bottle, ran up an enormous bar bill, before returning home to the Midlands in the morning to fester and plan the next leg of this journey to end all journeys.

3: Upnor to Woolwich

Resuming my journey in the autumn of 2018, a few days after I finally retired from my university, at the ripe old age of sixty-nine, I drove down to Kent, all the way to Meopham Green, and called into the Cricketers pub for lunch. Although there was much memorabilia around the walls I was surprised that there was little evidence of any reference to our superior summer game, bearing in mind the importance of this location for the early development of cricket. I had a stroll around the triangular-shaped green opposite the pub which sported a well-tended square and noted the shortness of the boundaries in one or two spots, doubting now that this could be the venue for a serious game. After a short break I drove on to the Leather Bottle in Cobham via the undistinguished railway station provisioned settlement of Sole Street. When I arrived in Cobham, I parked up in the capacious Leather Bottle car park, but first, as had become my normal habit, I popped into the nearby Darnley Arms for a pint. I had a vicarious practise on the dartboard, finding that my left hand was almost as good as my right, before checking in. I found myself domiciled in the same front room, overlooking the street through leaded glass, that I had the year before. In the evening I remade my acquaintance with my namesake Brian, the landlord, and his staff.

In the bright new morning, I took a taxi back to the Kings Head pub in Upper Upnor where I left off last time. I set off enthusiastically for Lower Upnor along a cycleway under the high, forbidding walls of Upnor Castle and scrambled down some steep steps to emerge down by the River Medway. This castle is a fine example of an Elizabethan artillery fort developed 1599–1601 to protect warships anchored in the medieval dockyards at Chatham,

"I NOTED THE SHORTNESS OF THE BOUNDRIES IN ONE OR TWO SPOTS"

but, as previously stated, it singularly failed in this quest. The quintessential fort is best seen from the River Medway and is currently managed by English Heritage. Further on I noted two pubs facing onto the river: the Ship Inn and The Pier. There are fine views from here down the Medway estuary and across the river to Gillingham.

I trudged on past the Arethusa adventure centre for young people. The pub, The Pier, presumably refers to the pier to which the *Arethusa*, a former cadet training ship was once moored. I remember when I was just a lad being taken down to Allhallows on the Hoo Peninsula in the 1960s for a picnic on the front and the *Arethusa*, with its distinctive masts and rigging, being pointed out to me down on the shore. Indeed, I have an old photograph of me aged about four standing, somewhat reluctantly, on this very keyside in front of the ship. Researching this at home, I determined that there have been many ships over the years so called, named with a reference to a nymph in Greek mythology, who was transformed into a stream to escape the attentions of an amorous river god. The ship I remembered was actually a steel-hulled barque built in Hamburg, Germany in 1911 originally called the *Peking*, which was commissioned in 1933. Its purpose was to provide cadet training for boys from deprived parts of London through the Shaftsbury and Arethusa charity. This practice ceased in 1975 and the ship

N

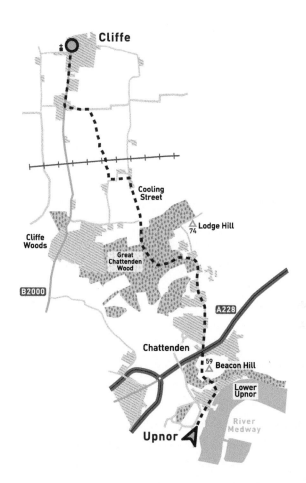

Cliffe

Cooling
Street

Lodge Hill
74

Cliffe
Woods

Great
Chattenden
Wood

B2000

A228

Chattenden

59
Beacon Hill

Lower
Upnor

River
Medway

Upnor

1km

was sold to a museum in New York and restored under its original name of the *Peking*. All that remains now is the onshore facilities of the training ship which I had just observed on this trip.

Me aged four standing on the quayside in front of the *Arethusa*

At this point I left the Saxon Shore Way and turned north, finding the local footpath to Beacon Hill. I climbed up through the trees, passing through an extensive open space on the side of the hill before reaching the summit. I came out on the main A228 road by two petrol garages and looked around for Chattenden Lane opposite. I sidled down the long, scruffy lane with army barracks and randomly developed housing strung out in ribbon fashion. I felt that with some decent planning an organised place could be created here in Chattenden, but as it stands there is no clear centre to this dormitory settlement. Rising all the time, the lane petered out in a redundant MOD site with copious warnings of the presence of unexploded devises and the footpath gradually evaporated. Frustrated, I retraced my steps and found a way back through Great Chattenden Wood, with the help of a local lady out walking her dogs. I climbed up and over the distinctive chalk ridge which runs down the centre of the Hoo Peninsula, reaching a maximum height of seventy-four metres on the nearby Lodge Hill.

I emerged from the gloomy wood by a sunny ninety-degree corner of an unfenced lane running down to Cooling Street. The area around Cliffe and Cooling has many of these right-angled bends in the road pattern, no doubt reflecting some historical field pattern. The flat plain on the northern side of the chalk ridge stretched gracefully all the way down to the Thames Estuary. I strolled down the lane to Cooling Street, turning west before the railway to pick up the bridleway into Cliffe. Then I doglegged across to the B2000, a seminal road number for quite an insignificant and undistinguished main road called Church Street, running from Wainscott north of Rochester down into the old centre of Cliffe. Whilst I understand that Cliffe was once a larger and more important settlement, I would have expected this road number to be reserved for a more significant route and this got me thinking about other seminal road numbers, such as the B1000 and the B3000. The B1000 is also a fairly insignificant route running from Welwyn Garden City to Hertford and the B3000 is a short stretch of road running south-west of Guildford. Warming to this game, I discovered the B4000 is a twenty-mile road in Berkshire which crosses the Vale of the White Horse. I concluded that the civil servant from the former Ministry of Transport who invented the road numbering system, based on the iconic map showing wedges of colour between A-roads emanating from London, was probably lacking in imagination on this point.

I plodded on down the street in the old part of Cliffe, with its white weather-boarded cottages and town houses clearly demonstrating their historical origins. The Black Bull, a former pub, at the bottom of the street was now a private residence. Pausing for a while by the steep little slope down onto the marsh, I imagined the sea water lapping at an ancient waterfront. I took the opportunity to have a look round St Helen's churchyard, a dedication to a popular Mercian saint of an original church founded by King Offa in 774. The current impressively large church was built in 1260 and is a testament of the importance of Cliffe, which was regarded as a town in the sixteenth century. I observed the charnel house, a Grade II listed building dating from the mid-nineteenth century, tucked away in a corner of the churchyard, which was used to store dead bodies dragged out of the River Thames. After digesting this macabre information, I retired to Six Bells for lunch before catching a taxi back to Cobham.

BRING IN YER DEAD!

"... WHICH WAS USED TO STORE DEAD BODIES DRAGGED OUT OF THE THAMES"

The next day I returned to Cliffe to resume my endless journey. I walked out down the old street, evocative of past glories in the much-diminished town, to the flat plain that stretched out in front, aiming for the big river. I turned left underneath a charming farm complex with attractive barns which once would have been on the coast when Cliffe was in its heyday. It reminded me very much of the farm complex at Lower Woolwich, near Tenterden, overlooking the Rolvenden Channel, again once an inlet of the sea. Looking back, I observed the steep little rise at the bottom of the slope from another angle, which would have kept the waters out of the town. The steep little rise reminded me of that same landscape feature in the village of Oare near Faversham or Appledore on the margins of Romney Marsh. Looking out across the marshes to the River Thames, I could not help but see massive container ships with nodding derricks moored on the other side of the river at Thames Haven. They looked like substantial buildings on the skyline with red container bricks piled high.

I ambled out of Cliffe under a ten-metre-high chalk cliff of the Francis quarry, named after Alfred Francis, who started a cement business here in 1860. This injection of Victorian enterprise to some extent revived the fortunes of the town until the closure of the quarry in 1920. The chalk was excavated by hand and the quarry became famous for producing valuable fossils. As a consequence, the quarry has been designated as a regionally important geological site, protected under planning law in the guise of geological conservation.

Map 12: Cliffe to Cobham

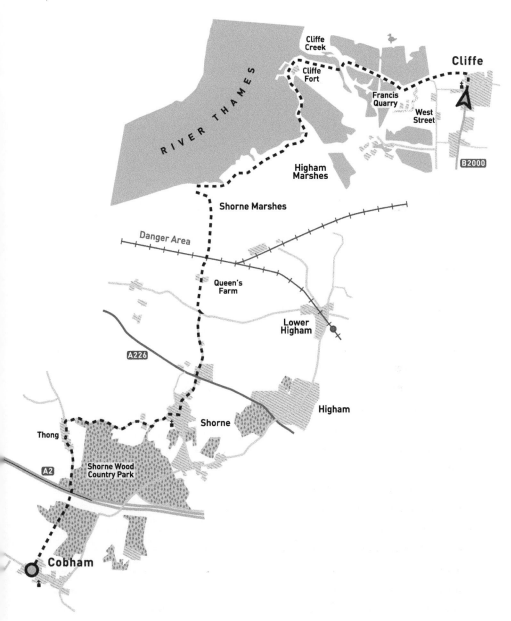

On my right was a massive body of water created by gravel extraction, a legacy of the current enterprise operating in the vicinity. These, the Cliffe Pools, are a 1,730-acre RSPB nature reserve acquired in 2001. I could clearly see the work that had been carried out to shallow the pools and create lagoons and islands to produce a conducive habitat for water birds. I could see many birds in the distance but, not having my binoculars handy, I could not tell what make they were. I came to a scruffy junction, damaged by lorries associated with the gravel workings, where there was a confusing plethora of footpaths. According to a rather obscure notice, one way was evidently closed but it was difficult to ascertain which one. I took the Saxon Shore Way out along a narrow, raised bank between two massive sheets of shallow water towards Cliffe Fort on the banks of the Thames Estuary. Gradually, with a sinking feeling, realising that not many walkers had passed this way, the walking became more and more difficult. Eventually I had to gingerly push my way through thickets of blackthorn redolent with ripe sloes, vicious thorns and head-high arching brambles. Then, to cap it all, I came to a stream where the bridge had clearly collapsed and was now missing. I seriously considered turning back here but the thought of struggling back through the blackthorn-infested path spurred me on. I managed to cross over the stream by shuffling along two parallel clay pipes about a foot in diameter which would have originally run under the bridge. I hate to think about the predicament I would have been in if I had slipped off these pipes and plummeted into the muddy ditch below. Clearly the notice I had observed earlier referred to this path, the Saxon Shore Way. I felt the footpath closure could have been made much clearer.

At Cliffe Creek, there is a dogleg on the Saxon Shore Way, and on the southern side of the creek the way was virtually impassable. I carried on slowly, being sucked in further and further in the vain hope that I would emerge on a clear path. The only reason to carry on was to avoid the thought of retracing my steps. Approaching the gravel workings, with its pyramidal piles of discarded yellow sand, the path was completely obliterated and I had to carefully pick my way round precarious unstable slopes at the base of these hills, across muddy lagoons and damp ditches. Eventually I managed to gain access to the raised riverbank and coastal path, and took a deep breath, grateful that this challenging, if somewhat foolhardy, traverse had been successfully negotiated. Clearly something has to be done to repair the Saxon Shore Way in this vicinity, an important national long-distance footpath.

Having reached the coastal path, safely elevated on the riverbank, I reflected on the experience before walking on. Whilst I can appreciate the winning of materials such as gravel and sand are vital to our modern civilisation, necessary for a vast range of construction activities, gravel workings do make a complete mess of the landscape. In this case, the gravel workings had completely obliterated the footpath. However, thereafter the expansive sheet of shallow water left after the dredging has ceased, can and often are reclaimed for wildlife and recreational habitats. Having reached the banks of the River Thames, I proceeded westwards through the aforesaid earthy enterprise. I passed underneath spidery extraction contraptions by a specially created walkway to protect the Saxon Shore Way. Clearly at some time in the past these arrangements had been agreed with the concern operating the gravel workings; I thought it a shame that this enlightened attitude had not percolated down to current times and the obvious damage down to the Saxon Shore Way over the section I had just negotiated.

Passing through the gravel workings, I came to the massive waterlogged ruins of Cliffe Fort. I took a photograph of the derelict but still impressive structure completely overgrown, inaccessible and flooded. Again, I couldn't help but feel that the condition of this thameside fort was also due to the adjacent gravel extraction works. I skirted round the fort and was relieved to be clear of all this mayhem. I passed the prototype torpedo shoot associated with the fort, that I have remarked on before in a previous book, appearing now to be more damaged by tidal erosion than when I last visited. Clearly this historic monument, which is included in English Heritage's 'at risk' register, is in a dire condition, but on the face of it, I'm not sure what one could do with it. What would be the purpose of restoring it as it is completely inaccessible, marooned as it is, out on the marshes, to anybody but intrepid ramblers like me?

Carrying on, I came to another place where the footpath was closed, but I didn't believe it could be any worse than the hazards I had just negotiated, so I carried on regardless. In a number of places, the bank on which the path was set had been eaten by the sea, but I just hopped around the edge of each greedy bite. I came across a damp, swampy thicket where evidently one had to be aware of the danger posed by adders. Over the years of trekking around Kent, I have come across such warning notices on a number of occasions, demonstrating that the occurrence of our one shy, poisonous snake is perhaps more common than one would expect. However, having said that, I have never seen a live adder, but I did see a dead one many years ago on the cliffs above Cheddar Gorge in Somerset. I continued trekking west beside the bleak estuary, gazing on the prospect of the light grey river, until I located the footpath across the reclaimed marshes to Shorne.

I fell in with two birdwatchers walking away from the nearby Shorne Marshes bird sanctuary to the east of Gravesend and crossed the flat marshes on a footpath I had taken before. As I approached the railway, along the back edge of the marshes, I disturbed a charm of goldfinches, sending them flitting between bushes, and passed a field which was home to some friendly cart horses. Indeed, the more sheltered back of the marsh seemed to be more populated with wildlife; it reminded me of Minnsmere in Suffolk, where I had observed marsh harriers from a discreetly located hide.

My passage across the railway at the back of the marsh was delayed by an extremely long goods train carrying railway sleepers backing slowly into a nearby siding in which, I guess, there was a large railway works. I think this was unusual because we are accustomed to large trains going forwards, not backwards, and to be honest it never occurred to me that such trains could back up in this way. I was delayed by about ten minutes, fascinated by this curious manoeuvre before negotiating the surface crossing. In the lane past Queen's Farm, I observed many scruffy and extensive enterprises typified by scrapyards. I slogged up the lane to the dogleg on the Gravesend to Lower Higham road and on up past Green Farm to the A226. Rising all the time, I struggled up the lane to Shorne village and took lunch in the Rose and Crown pub. I recall last time I was here I had a very affable lunchtime talking to locals at the bar. This time, no conversation was forthcoming, but nevertheless it was a pleasant enough experience. I have found that it is a risky business to revisit places where a good time was had, expecting the inevitable disappointment with the repeat experience.

The next day I decided to have a day off walking and to explore the Hoo Peninsula and the Isle of Grain. I drove out of Cobham and along the narrow winding road to Shorne Ridgeway in the morning murk. I pressed on through Higham and tried to join the A289 at Wainscott, but there was a huge backlog of traffic, which I understand was due to a serious accident on the nearby A2. So, I cut my losses, turned the car round in the road and headed north to Cliffe Woods. I carried on to Cliffe and took the back route through the sinuous lanes through Cooling to High Halstow and down to Fenn Street along quiet lanes that I had walked before. I noticed that the Fenn Bell Inn, which was closed when I last passed, was now thankfully open. It was much too early for a drink, so I pressed on to the unremarkable coastal village of Allhallows-on-Sea, a place I had, in my first book, vowed never to revisit. I had a look round the elemental, almost feudal village of St Mary Hoo on the way and noted once again the church, some pleasant dwellings and the integral Moat Farm. As before, arriving in Allhallows-on-Sea, I noted that the beach front had been appropriated by a massive holiday park. I drove inland to the original settlement of All Hallows and on to Lower Stoke. Here I stopped for petrol at a run-down garage and was, with old-fashioned charm and a curtesy, served petrol by an attractive East European lady.

From Lower Stoke I took the A228 to the isolated village of Grain at the apex of the Hoo Peninsula. In the process I had to cross the low-lying marsh, which used to be the Yantlet Creek, once a channel of open water giving access from the Thames to the River Medway and the Swale. In days gone by, Grain, or to give it its other name, St James, was actually an island at the far extremity of the Hoo Peninsula. Then I passed down along a long, straight road through an industrial area dominated by the National Grid, although the nearby power station is defunct. Coming into the village, I drove on down past the church, dedicated to the same saint, and parked up by the beach. I sat for a while, gazing out into the Thames Estuary, all the way across to Shoeburyness in Essex. The sun and tide were out, and peace descended on me. One of those special quiet moments only accompanied by squabbling seagulls down on the beach and the tinnitus in my right ear.

Strolling around the head, I met two lady walkers who were intent on tackling the Saxon Shore Way. We exchanged pleasantries and I was able to furnish them with a flyer about my third book, in which they seemed genuinely interested. Afterwards I rued the fact that I did not warn them of the perils that lay before them in the vicinity of Cliffe Fort. I explored the Country Park and noticed the remnants of Grain Fort, known as The Maze and Grain tower, out in the Medway Estuary. This fort and tower, together with Garrison Fort in Sheerness, just over the water at this point, were built in the 1860s to guard the Medway Estuary from attack in one of many periods of tension with France. Looking over the river to Sheerness, I could see the masts of the SS *Richard Montgomery* sticking out of the water, a sunken American ship from the Second World War carrying a massive cargo of munitions. Evidently the state of these unstable explosive devises under the water is constantly being monitored but it is said if they were ever to explode, the tidal wave created would completely swamp the Isle of Grain. I was mildly impressed by the beach and front at Grain poking out into the Thames Estuary; it had a remote atmosphere and I would doubt whether it ever got crowded. After an hour or so taking in the scene, I drove back up the main street to the Hogarth Inn. William Hogarth, that famous English painter of the eighteenth-century, evidently visited the Isle of Grain with his merry gang on a perambulation through North Kent. I spent a pleasant lunch chatting to the landlord and landlady about the history of the Inn, the second oldest building in the village after the church.

Next morning, I returned to Shorne and walked up the steep footpath past the church to pick up the lane to the hamlet of Upper Ifield. This was a twisty undulating lane with steep little rises across the grain of the land that I had walked before, the other way from Gravesend into Shorne. To my right the flat lands spread out down to the big river. I joined the north/south lane through Thong, a small, well kept hamlet on the outskirts of Gravesend. I noted the lovely flint and brick walls lining the street that adds so much character; the same as I had observed in Cobham. Skirting the edge of Shorne Woods Country Park I came up to the junction with the A2, a massively busy road. I crossed over the road and the adjacent railway and proceeded down the side of the heavily coppiced Ashenbank Wood; an open access area managed by the excellent Woodland Trust. As is usual in these situations, the wood was grazed by cattle to keep the wood from reaching its climax state; a dense, impenetrable cover of woodland. I liberated sweet chestnuts from their spiky cases by an adroit application of a stamping foot. Luckily the bitter pith came away easily and the raw nuts, much better in my opinion than when roasted, were delicious. I have noticed that these nuts, traditionally saved up until Christmas, have often gone bad, often infested with wriggly maggots and when roasted, impossible to part with their bitter pith, making them virtually inedible.

I noted that in this vicinity north and east of Cobham there was little arable farmland. The area was largely given over to recreational pursuits with woods and some rough pasture supporting the inevitable horse paddocks. The reserves included: Shorne Woods Country Park, Ashenbank Wood, Jeskyns Country Park, Cobham Park, and Great Wood and Ranscombe Farm Nature Reserve. This constitutes a plethora of opportunities for the citizens of Gravesend and the Medway Towns to get out and enjoy the countryside. As I approached the back of Cobham by an orchard, the sun came out strongly. I crossed over a recreational ground, gained access to the car park of the Leather Bottle and passed under an impressive eucalyptus arch belonging to the pub, before retrieving my car and passing on to my next destination. I actually drove on to Southfleet on a recce, having lunch in the Ship Inn there. Then I drove on to the Black Prince, a now holiday inn in Old Bexley. This former roadhouse holds many childhood memories for me; of stops in trips back from the coast in my grandfather's car, of which I have remarked on before. But the Black Prince, a much-lauded knight, and son and heir of Edward III, who served with distinction in the Hundred Years' War with France, evidently stayed in the nearby Hall Place across the road, before embarking for the continent from which he never returned; an event now celebrated in the name of the adjacent road interchange on the A2. In the evening I had a stroll around Old Bexley, revisiting a number of well-remembered liquid emporiums.

I made an early start on Saturday morning because heavy rain was promised later. I drove on to Cobham in the early morning mist. Parking up in the Leather Bottle again, I strolled out of Cobham westwards, past Owletts, a National Trust property and once the home of the famous architect Sir Herbert Baker (1862–1946), who was born and died in this grand house. He worked with Lutyens in New Delhi and extensively in South Africa but is evidently largely disregarded today. From the hamlet of Jeskyns, I plodded across a massive, open, ploughed field towards Ifield Court. This was a very strange experience because in the mist I was walking blind for at least half a mile. I had traversed this footpath before, going the other way, so I had some idea of where I was headed and was able to follow infrequent footprints in the soil like tracking an animal in some wild nature adventure. I passed under an electricity power line humming mournfully in the mist, gaining a degree of reassurance that I was on the right track.

Map 13: Cobham to Darenth

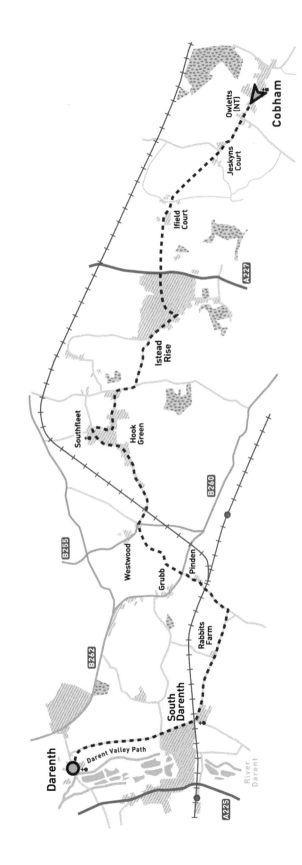

1km

Making the corner of the field I crossed over the lane and carried on around the back of the historic Ifield Court, a Grade II listed building consisting of a Georgian house built onto a fifteenth-century manor house. Needless to say, being diverted around the back of this residence I was not able to admire its splendour. As the mist began to lift, I crossed over the Wealdway near its northern terminus in Gravesend and continued on under a phalanx of electricity pylons and came up to the main A227 road, the same road that I had been toying with for many miles and several years in my northern progress through Kent. I crossed over the road into the relatively modern settlement of Istead Rise. Walking through modern houses, there was indeed a steep rise in Istead Rise, a place clearly living up to its name. At the top of the rise I popped into a local Co-op for rations. Then, after picking up the back road, there was an interminable, unappealing slog up to a height of fifty-four metres, near the junction with the next lane. In a field corner I observed of flock of brown game birds which preferred to float across the surface of the field at my approach rather than taking off in flight. I thought they might be woodcocks but I'm not sure. There was a footpath to the right cutting off the corner at the junction, but it was impassable due to a mature crop of sweetcorn.

After a short stretch of lane northwards towards Northfleet, I found the lane down into Southfleet at a junction by a decorative pond graced by many ducks. The entrance to the village was through an attractive grouping of buildings which I guess would have been a separately named hamlet in the past. Then I passed some nondescript houses infilling the area before the main attractive historic heart of the village around the church and pub. This village is twinned geographically with Northfleet, a place I confess having never visited, on the Thames Estuary. I imagine there is a River Fleet, but I could see no sign of it on the ground. I reached the Ship Inn too early for lunch, so after a quick look round, I ordered a taxi to take me back to Cobham where I had left my car. I retreated to my base in Old Bexley village as the rain set in with a vengeance.

Next morning, a Sunday, I returned to Southfleet and walked out on the rising lane through Hook Green to the sound of church bells, passing Friary Court, another Grade II listed building, in the process. Looking back towards the church in the village across the fields, I could see right down to the river. There were pylons everywhere, marching across the landscape, with cables slung between. I was struck by the backdrop to the church; an industrial landscape, dominated in the past by cement manufacture, stretching down to the River Thames. The legacy of this industry shows up in a series of massive chalk quarries, one of which accommodates the out-of-town shopping complex that is Bluewater. I have to confess here that I have never been to Bluewater and to be honest would rather not go in the future. Somehow this shopping centre covering 240 acres, the fifth largest in the UK, seems to exert a subtle gravitational pull on people's minds and the surrounding area, but I was determined to resist its undoubted charms. Southfleet is just in the country, south of the A2 and no doubt a welcome escape for people from Dartford, Gravesend, Greenhithe, Swanscombe and Northfleet. From this vantage point my gaze northwards crossed the site of Vagniacis, on the B259 out of Swanscombe, a major Roman settlement on Watling Street recently excavated by Wessex Archaeology.

"THERE WERE PYLONS EVERYWHERE MARCHING ACROSS THE LANDSCAPE, WITH CABLES SLUNG BETWEEN THEM"

I crossed under the power lines again, as common round here as petrol stations, and over the railway line. I started to think about these disfiguring utilities that littered the landscape around here, converging on the Northfleet Power Station on the banks of the River Thames. Researching at home, I discovered that this power station was decommissioned in 1991, and therefore one is inclined to ask the question: what purpose do all these overhead lines now serve if they don't carry any electricity? Clearly the authorities have not thought to remove the redundant infrastructure blighting the landscape. In fact, I would go as far as saying that I have never heard of redundant electricity pylons being removed from the landscape. Maybe my concern here is misplaced and that the cables are still in use, the electricity supply merely being re-routed from other sources, but it would be interesting to find out whether the continued existence of all these pylons is justified and whether some rationalisation of the infrastructure would be appropriate.

Coming up to the junction with the B255, I admired a classic former thatched pub on the corner which had been converted to a no doubt commodious residence. Searching for the footpath across the fields to Grubb Street, I got caught up in a stable complex with friendly horses who demanded to be stroked. I waved across the paddocks to a stable girl looking after the horses. Coming out of this untidy equine enclave, I got diverted further south, missing the direct footpath to Grubb Street. Instead I crossed under overhead power lines again and came up to the B260 opposite the lane to Pinden. It is always reassuring, when following a footpath, to see that others had already walked that way, as was the case with this footpath. It gives one the confidence to believe that the path would lead somewhere and not just peter out. I came up hard against a quarry searching for a path down to the next lane. Scrambling up and over a steep bank, I crossed diagonally across a field, where I observed a group of shaggy inkcap mushrooms doing their stuff, spreading their spores around. When I reached the gate at the far edge of the field, the sign on the reverse side said 'Danger'. I concluded that I had turned too soon and potentially risked life and limb skirting the edge of the quarry, maybe through a landfill site. I carried on down across the field, aiming for the far corner where I knew from my map that the footpath met the lane below. It was a lovely day for walking in the cool air and brightly shining sun.

I took the sinuous lane opposite between immaculately kept hedges which led to the equally immaculately kept hamlet of Pinden to the west of Longfield. Passing out under a monumental brick railway arch, I started a slow ascent. As I climbed I mused on the proposition that it would be helpful to walkers if footpaths were classified, much like roads. I felt it would be beneficial to define strategic paths, thereby distinguishing these useful paths from local footpaths. Many local footpaths were more fluid, responding to changing local needs and used mainly for dog walking. I felt that such paths could be non-statutory, thereby concentrating scarce resources in looking after the more important strategic paths. Clearly bridleways would generally fall within the strategic category as well as designated long-distance footpaths. I have also proposed in the past that more strategic paths could be created and even imagined a new bridleways Act of Parliament to facilitate this process, but maybe it can already achieved under current legislation. As I climbed up past Rabbit's Farm at a height of eighty-eight metres, I observed a profusion of old man's beard, a wild version of clematis, scrambling through the hedgerow.

In time I came to the junction by Southdowns church at the entrance to what appeared to be a private estate above the Darenth Valley. Before crossing over the railway line to my right, I tarried for a while, leaning on a gate, looking down on the splendid prospect of the valley laid out below. To my left I could see Horton Kirby church across the fields and recalled a cricket match in the village where my team had been soundly beaten. The last time I had walked along this valley was in the summer of 2001, on a trek from Dartford to Sevenoaks along the Darent Valley Path recorded in Book 1, a mere seventeen years ago. I spent an engaging five minutes chatting to a local bloke out walking his dog, swopping information and experiences of the valley below before crossing over the railway and walking out across the back of South Darenth. Here I was favourably struck by the string of modest houses fronting the road in which the ordinary working people of this vicinity lived. I was generously disported to a socialist world of honourable working people. I skipped along a pavement punctuated by loaded parking bays. Further on I entered Roman Villa Road, a reminder of the extensive Roman settlement of this pleasant valley.

I elected to take the high road, a small lane on the map, which I anticipated would give stunning views of the valley below, which it did. However, the narrow lane, with damaged passing places carved out of the banks by frequent traffic, was perilous walking and it was hard to enjoy the view. Evidently the ordinary working people of this vicinity, using this lane as a shortcut, had inadvertently largely destroyed it; a metaphor, perhaps, for our current social circumstances. I had to hurry from passing place to passing place to avoid the oncoming flurries of cars rushing by. From time to time, when two cars driving in opposite directions could not pass in the narrow lane, I was able to witness a number of bad-tempered stand-offs. The one thing that was quite clear to me was that in walking this lane I was an unwelcome addition to this mayhem. It was as if the message sent to me was that I had no right to walk along this racetrack. To add the final insult, many of the laybys were blessed with piles of rubbish, dumped presumably by the very same hard-working locals eulogised earlier. I observed a field down in the valley where model aeroplanes were being put through their paces. Why it was necessary for one of these replicas to strafe me I'm not sure, except that no doubt this episode caused considerable amusement to the grounded pilot. Keen to escape these unkindly thoughts and regain my mood, finally, I was glad to find a footpath diagonally across a ploughed field down to Darenth church, cutting off the corner with the next lane.

"THE ONE THING THAT WAS CLEAR TO ME WAS THAT WALKING IN THIS LANE
I WAS AN UNWELCOME ADDITION TO THIS MAYHEM"

I stood outside the church, dedicated to St Margaret of Antioch, a strange connection with modern-day Turkey. Antioch was once a major centre of the early Christian church roughly halfway between Istanbul and Jerusalem, which probably explains the dedication. As for Margaret, she was martyred for refusing to marry a Roman governor, giving rise to numerous apparent miracles resulting in her elevation to the curious status of sainthood. Her plight seems well appreciated now, as over 250 churches are dedicated to her, including Westminster, the parish church of the Houses of Parliament. I rested for a while and pondered on Darenth as a place. Last time I passed through, I was rather scathing about this ancient village and determined to revisit to see if my first impressions were correct. Standing in front of the church, on the busy road down the hill from the large housing estate on the eastern side of the B260, I saw nothing to change my mind.

I crossed over the road and strolled down the remaindered lane opposite to find the Chequers pub down by the river. My first impression of the frontage was of an old, somewhat neglected building in a scruffy lane. The landlady admitted me early, before official opening time, and showed considerable hospitality. I had a pleasant lunch sitting at the bar before the pub became crowded out on this Sunday lunchtime. I strolled out into the garden and regarded the waters of the River Darenth flowing strongly down to Dartford. After an agreeable interlude, I went outside into the lane and ordered a taxi to take me back to my base in Bexley village. The sun was shining now and the pub was lit up, greatly improving its appeal. It was bought to my attention in the pub that the lane on which I was standing once went all the way into Dartford. Checking my map, I could clearly see that the lane was brutally truncated by the construction of the major road intersection of the A2 and the M25/A282 leading down to the Dartford crossing. I felt the landlady had done well to run a clearly successful pub on what now was a serious backwater. Even the taxi driver had trouble finding the pub and I spent a good forty minutes lolling around outside in the heavily parked up lane waiting for it to arrive. In spite of the remoteness of the pub, it is thankfully on the Darent Valley Path and would no doubt afford solace for ramblers like me. However, last time I walked down the Darent Valley, I managed to miss this pub, because I recall I used the main road, having failed to find the footpath out of Dartford after the A2. That time, I crossed back over the river and rejoined the Darent Valley Path just west of the church.

Thus ended this leg from Upnor to Darenth, and I returned to Birmingham determined to return in the spring and finish this particular walk at my birthplace of Woolwich on the River Thames in south-east London before my seventieth birthday. I imagined walking once again across Dartford Heath to Crayford and out on the marshes to Erith. Then, picking up the Thames Path, I would walk along the mighty river, past Thamesmead on to Woolwich.

I returned to Kent early in the year, before Easter, the earliest time of year that I had ever walked, to finish off this marathon journey. I drove down to Dartford, where I stayed in the splendid Royal Victoria & Bull Hotel at number 1 High Street. This former coaching inn on the main A2 Rochester Way, Watling Street, in Roman times, a listed building, still showed the gallery where horse-drawn coaches would have pulled in. Access to the pub was via an elaborate car park associated with the Priory shopping centre to the rear of the pub. I arrived just in time to watch a Premier League football match between Arsenal and Watford on the giant screen in the concourse, before retiring to my room. In the early evening, I explored again the town where once I worked in the council offices as a trainee town planner. I was struck by the number of derelict buildings and vacant plots in the High Street and concluded that Dartford may have fallen on hard times. Talking to a chap in the Malt Shovel pub, he was in no doubt that the cause was the large influx of Polish and Romanian immigrants; a sentiment I could not lightly share.

In the morning I caught a taxi that took me back to St Margaret's church in Darenth. I set off down the hill towards the River Darent, which in this vicinity is a bifurcated stream with large sheets of open water between each arm. Crossing over the Darent Valley path that I had traipsed along many years ago, I strolled on down Parsonage Lane past Sutton Place up to the main A225. Evidently Sutton Place was once a Tudor mansion of great note and magnificence, now demolished. I observed the only remaining vestige of this edifice in the listed and striking Tudor garden wall facing the lane. Opposite the ancient brick wall was a field with attractive horses, most of whom were milling about, but a few were lying down in a most ungainly fashion. I don't think I had ever seen horses lying down like this and I did wonder whether they would actually manage to get up without assistance. Crossing over the main road, I strolled up the lane towards the M25. Immediately after the motorway I searched for a footpath across the fields to Wilmington. The footpath I was looking for had been ploughed away and I trudged down a field edge to end up in the lane by Hawley. The light brown soil was littered with flint nodules liberated from the underlying chalk strata. The importance of this humble rock in the evolution of mankind cannot be underestimated, its origin being the subject of considerable academic debate.

From the corner of the lane lined with utilitarian bungalows I trekked across the back of Hawley. I remembered cycling down this lane with my schoolfriend and enjoying an exhilarating freewheel career down the slope into the Darent valley. Now, looking back over the valley, I was struck by the number of glasshouses glinting in the morning sun. I found a footpath inside the field's edge and struck out across another massive ploughed field towards Wilmington. Here I observed a skylark hovering in the sky and tweeting above me. Again, the footpaths shown on the map in this vicinity had been completely ploughed away. However, the local farmer had created new paths between blocks of carefully prepared ground where the soil had been earthed up in strips ready for planting. In the corner of the field was a massive watering contraption creating a charming rainbow through the fine mist that it exuded. I came into the edge of Wilmington by a track hard up against the roaring A2 and turned west towards the centre of Wilmington.

Although once a small village, Wilmington now forms an undistinguished southerly extension of Dartford effectively cut in two by the A2 Dartford bypass constructed in 1973. At the crossroads in the centre of the village, I observed an interesting quartered village sign and popped into the corner shop for water and chocolate. I carried on past The Foresters, a redundant pub, and slid down the lane, past the local grammar schools that led up to the common. Wilmington Common is really a southerly extension of Dartford Heath, sliced off by the same A2 road. I crossed over at Leyton Cross and took the Heath Road before striking out across the heath towards Crayford. The gorse bushes were in fine form and the silver birches' graceful fronds were about to burst into leaf. This 314-acre expanse of the distinctly rare habitat of lowland heath, designated as an Area of Outstanding Natural Beauty, is much used by dog walkers. I was aiming for the roundabout in the centre of the heath and discovered a disused gravel pit where I remembered years ago coming off my bike while trying to negotiate a particularly steep slope. I succeeded in scraping my cheek, a contusion that created a scar which was to stay with me for many years.

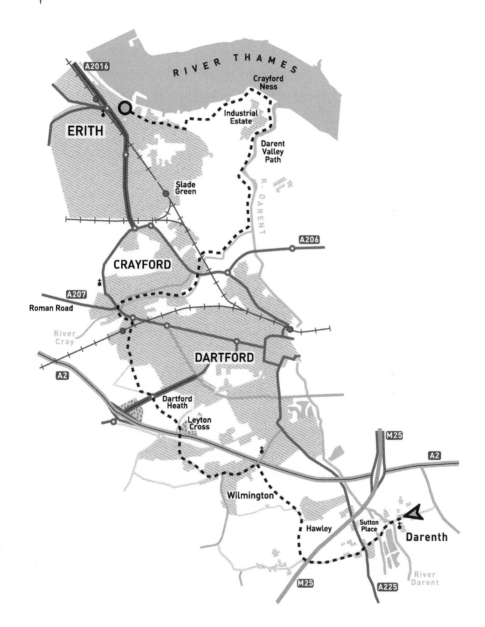

N

RIVER THAMES

A2016

Crayford
Ness

ERITH

Industrial
Estate

Darent
Valley
Path

Slade
Green

R. DARENT

A206

CRAYFORD

A207

Roman Road

River
Cray

DARTFORD

A2

Dartford
Heath

Leyton
Cross

M25

A2

Wilmington

Hawley

Sutton
Place

Darenth

M25

A225

River
Darent

1km

Crossing the main road at the junction, I strode on along a short stretch of road called Rochester Way, the same as where I lived for many years further west at 897 in Welling. I carried on further across the heath on a wooded path parallel to Swan Lane on the way to Crayford. I passed by a large recreation area and although the heath is named after Dartford, in my view it belongs as much to Crayford. Carrying on down the hill past some pleasant houses bordering the common, I passed under the railway and came into Crayford town centre. I expected Crayford to be much like Dartford, but it wasn't: there was no sign of urban dereliction. On the contrary, Crayford seemed a thriving town centre in the London borough of Bexley. After a quick look around and grabbing a bite to eat, I caught the bus down Watling Street, back to Dartford for rest and recuperation. Strolling down West Hill, I popped into the Royal Oak for a lunchtime drink. In the evening I continued my exploration of Dartford, calling in the historic Wat Tyler pub down by the river. Wat Tyler reputedly passed this way leading the Peasants' Revolt in 1381 on his way to his death in London town at the hands of Richard II.

The next day I returned to Crayford and picked up the Cray Valley Walk northward out onto the marshes. Trudging alongside the River Cray on a scruffy path across the backs of houses and industrial premises, I made good progress. On reaching the A206 I had to detour away from the river to skirt around a large industrial estate. Coming back to the river with the marshes ahead, I observed starlings and very tame grey wagtails bobbing about on the tarmac, which for some reason seems to be a preferred habitat. In this location the river had widened out, with the stream bed being choked by a host of tall, yellow reeds. It felt very remote out here plodding along the riverside path and I could clearly see the Dartford crossing; the Queen Elizabeth II Bridge, built in 1991 to supplement existing tunnels, elegantly spanning the River Thames to my right. In time I came to the confluence of the rivers Cray and Darent and noted the rivers appeared to be tidal at this point. Approaching Crayford Ness, I skirted round a large industrial estate, home to an extensive car breakers yard with hundreds of dead lorries parked up and rusting away. Surrounding the estate was an area of rough pasture grazed by a large number of apparently wild horses. At the mouth of the Darent, where it joins the Thames, there is a massive concrete edifice housing sluice gates, which were built in 1981 to prevent floodwater reaching Dartford and Crayford. This stretch of the River Darent is known as Dartford Creek and in times past, barges used to ply upstream to service the industries of the two towns before they were swamped in London sprawl. Looking across the river from the point, I could make out Purfleet in Essex and an enormous, incongruous concave mound which I guessed was a major landfill site for London's rubbish.

Pressing on to Erith, I skirted around an impressive marina filled with yachts of various sizes and was channelled away from the waterfront through another gloomy industrial estate, before emerging in the town centre. This riverside town is the birthplace of Wendy Cope, an engaging poet whom I have quoted in my first volume of walks entitled *Finding My Place*. As I arrived, I saw my bus waiting at the terminus and so I jumped on and returned to Dartford, foregoing my intended perusal of Erith. From a cursory glance from the bus, Erith town centre appeared to be a shabby reminder of 1960's too optimistic flat roof retail developments. The tortuous journey wound through Slade Green to Crayford before going on to Dartford. After taking lunch in the Royal Victoria & Bull and changing out of walking boots, I drove on to Woolwich, my next berth. I passed through Bexleyheath and at Welling corner I turned down Wickham Lane to Plumstead; a journey down memory lane. All that remained now was to locate the Travelodge in Woolwich where I was staying for a couple of nights.

I found a car park at the derelict end of Powys Street and booked into the Travelodge after negotiating complex parking arrangements. After a short rest, I explored Woolwich for the first and probably the last time; the place where I was born. I strolled down the pedestrianised Powys Street to Beresford Square and observed the former entrance gate to the Royal Woolwich Arsenal. The important role of this armaments factory over the centuries cannot be overstated and the factory also was the birthplace of Arsenal football club, currently one of the most prominent teams in the Premier League. I ate in a wimpy bar and had a drink in the Earl of Chatham and the Castle Inn at the top of Powys street, before returning to my functional room. In the dilapidated Castle Inn, I was served by oriental bar staff in a pub graced solely by the local Afro-Caribbean community.

In the morning, after breakfast, I caught a 99 bus back to Erith to complete this marathon trek, possibly my last ever day of serious walking. It was a lovely, fine sunny day; quite remarkable for this time of year. Disembarking in the uninspiring town centre I elected to take the Thames

Path west out of Erith, which I knew would be well signposted. I passed out via a grand, monumental roundabout and some new riverside apartments before coming on to the big river. Striding on past industrial premises all the way up to Jenningtree Point, I passed under many overhead gantries connecting gravel and cement workings to jetties out in the river. I'm not sure how many of these conveyor contraptions are in active use, the bulk goods produced still being shipped out down the river. I noticed a group of shelducks making one of these jetties their home. Across the magnificent river I could see the famous Ford car factory at Dagenham.

Bending round the point into Halfway Reach, I ambled past a large new power station, called Riverside Resource Recovery, making energy from waste, a new highly technical facility. Next in this westward perambulation I came across an area of waste ground that had been converted into a nature reserve. I spotted a heron standing statuesque by the riverside on the edge of an extensive area of reed beds. I came to a second power station of an equally advanced technology built in fantastical shapes and colours. Observing an amazing array of birds, including various ducks and herons and a host of brown birds, populating a small promontory sticking out into the river, I reflected on the fact that there must now be sufficient fish in the River Thames to sustain this colony of herons; testament to the massive steps taken to clean up the river, now one of the cleanest major European rivers.

Then I came to a modern sewage works, one of the largest in Europe evidently, the premises of which accommodated the original Victorian buildings of the Crossness Pumping Station. This famous old pumping station, engineered by Sir Joseph Bazalgette and designed by the architect Charles Henry Driver, was opened in 1865 to deal with a severe sewage problem building up in London town, the most downriver outfall of eighty-two miles of underground sewer network serving the capital. It was now an industrial museum and Grade I listed building and noted for its extravagant cathedral-like interior.

There were some well-designed dwellings along the riverside by the massive dormitory of Thamesmead, most of which is built upon grounds associated with the former Woolwich Arsenal. This riverside walk through Barking Reach was faceted with concrete against the river and I paused frequently, leaning on the balustrade, just to gaze on the river and admire its insistent fluid might and majesty. Walking across the back of Woolwich Arsenal, the river reverted to a natural foreshore up to Tripcock Ness. Turning into Gallions Reach and

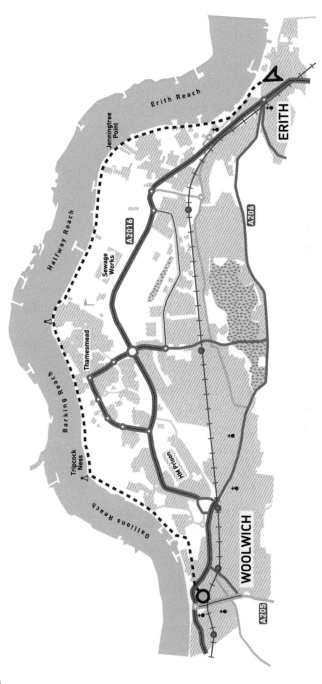

N

1km

approaching Woolwich, there were many expensive-looking riverside apartments. Thamesmead was really a much bigger township than I remembered when I last visited in the late sixties. Being a town planning student, I had walked from my home in Welling across Plumstead Common and down to Abbey Wood, to observe the much-vaunted early developments in Thamesmead. I remembered walking down beside a large lake, the same that featured in a notorious scene in the film *A Clockwork Orange*, fronted by shuffled apartments with car parking underneath; an arrangement supposed to protect against possible flooding. From the riverside walk, the spectacle was not unpleasing, although from comments made to me in the hotel the night before I was led to believe that parts of Thamesmead had lost its sparkle. I observed groups of African gentlemen lounging in the sun, sitting on convenient benches, ostensibly wasting time. I was reminded of the lyrics of 'Sittin' on the Dock of the Bay' by Otis Redding, thinking that this might be appropriate to their situation given that he sang about walking 2,000 miles from Georgia to the Frisco Bay. Some of these gentlemen may have travelled over 2,000 miles from their African homeland, unlike me, who has only walked the same distance over the years in Kent and East Sussex. As the planes roared overhead from the City Airport, I reflected on the sad fact that Otis died at the age of twenty-six in a plane crash.

Further on, approaching Woolwich, older buildings associated with the Arsenal, with distinctive grey-brown bricks, were incorporated into the riverside township and converted into residential dwellings. Strolling along by the river, it was hard to judge when I had reached the centre of Woolwich, which is set back from the riverside. There was no signage that I noticed which said 'town centre this way'. Reaching the guard houses associated with the former Arsenal, I decided to leave the riverside and sauntered down the monumental, tree-lined Number 1 Street, through the original heart of the Royal Woolwich Arsenal, feeling a little bit overwhelmed by the grandeur of the urban regeneration. Turning off to the right before the grand gatehouse in the foreground, I tried to gain access to the heritage museum which was supposed to be open but wasn't. I emerged onto the confusing, hectic High Street, which now effectively serves as the principal through route. Passing more massive riverside residential developments under construction, I came up to the centre via Hare Street. I grabbed another wimpy and a drink in the Earl of Chatham, one of the few remaining traditional pubs in Woolwich, before retiring to the hotel for a well-earned rest.

"Thus, three generations of my paternal family were intimately associated with Woolwich Arsenal"

In the evening I returned to Beresford Square and walked past the now slightly sad and isolated monumental gatehouse, to locate the main entrance to the Arsenal Riverside development. Strolling down Number 1 Street, I noted some posh restaurants and I had a satisfactory dinner in the Dial House, a converted building from the original Victorian Arsenal. I observed many focussed commuters streaming down from the station, some stopping off for an aperitif before returning to their new shiny apartments overlooking the magnificent river. It reminded me, sitting there in a state of reflection at the end of my travail, of lines from Eliot's *The Waste Land* about walking over London Bridge thus:

> '*I had not thought that death had done so many.*
> [Death's not the problem. Living is harder.]
> *Sighs, short and infrequent, were exhaled,*
> [OK, they had a hard day at work.]
> *And each man fixed his eyes before his feet.*
> [Careful not to stumble over the trendy cobbles.]'

This pathetic take-off of Wendy Cope's clever parody of T. S. Eliot in her verse entitled *Waste Land Limericks*, is an attempt to come to some sort of emotional conclusion of this journey. As I have previously intimated, the London energy of this location has not quite reached Erith, further downstream, Wendy's birthplace.

Continuing my perambulation around the town, it occurred to me that these city people were very different from the predominantly black community inhabiting the dilapidated top end of Powys Street where my berth was located. This evening, Woolwich very much felt like part of London; a contradiction of dereliction and redevelopment, an ethnic mix of regrettably separate communities. It felt also to me that the rural south-east country, however wonderful, that I had been walking through over many years, was little understood and very different from the real urban London, and populated by very few ethnic communities. South-east London was a place I had deserted more than forty years ago in search of an academic education, a way to clear my mind and learn how to think rationally about things. Coming back to Woolwich made me feel uncomfortable and seemed to challenge many of my perceptions. In spite of the distance I have travelled, I have never lost the essence of belonging to a working-class community now epitomised by the splendid black participants in Woolwich, at the top end of Powys Street.

Next morning, having completed my intended marathon journey, I took the morning out to have a look round Plumstead where many of my forebears lived while working in the Royal Woolwich Arsenal. I drove up and down a rather scruffy Plumstead High Street, searching for half-remembered landmarks. My father grew up in Plumstead before my grandparents moved out to Eltham and worked in the Arsenal until it closed in 1967. My grandad, Arthur William Charles Rance (1901–1986), also worked in the Arsenal and was born in Plumstead. The 1901 census shows my great-grandad, Arthur William Rance (1903–1967), who also worked in the Arsenal, was living at 68 Conway Road Plumstead aged twenty-one, with a recorded occupation as shell machinist, with his wife Lilian, a local girl from Abbey Wood aged nineteen. Thus, three generations of my paternal family were intimately associated with the Woolwich Arsenal. My great-uncle (great-grandfather's brother) Percival 'Percy' Rance (1877–1954) served as Labour mayor of Woolwich from 1937–38, just before the

Second World War. He and my great-grandad moved from the Victorian slums of Hitchin, Hertfordshire to work in the Woolwich Arsenal as young men. I find it strange that both my great-grandad and great-uncle were alive when I was growing up, clearly being significant members of the local community, but I can recall no mention of them within my family. Maybe my interest in moderate left-wing politics stems from this antecedence.

After looking around old Plumstead and noting the pleasant environment around the 100-acre common, which was protected as public open space in 1878 by an Act of Parliament, I drove on down Wickham Lane to Welling. Plumstead Common is basically a river terrace of our most recent geological period, when the waters of the ancient Thames poured out to an ice age River Rhine in what is now the North Sea. Arriving in Welling and slowly driving down the High Street, experiencing the fondly remembered places, much to the irritation of car drivers with a more urgent mission, I dallied erratically and parked up with insufficient notice. I would have taken time out to indulgently stroll down the High Street, if not for the well-intentioned local, in an accent I well-remembered, kindly telling me that I couldn't park in that spot. I headed her advice and passed on to Welling Way, out past the primeval Oxleas Woods where I picked up the A2 by Falconwood. I carried on past our old house at 897 Rochester Way, where I grew up, a fleeting farewell glimpse on the fast road, before picking up the M25 and making my way home to my adopted city, Birmingham. I have often wondered who might be living in that Wates-built 1930's suburban house now.

I couldn't help feeling a little sad on this seminal drive for two reasons: firstly, I felt it was unlikely I would ever have the time to return to my former stamping ground in south-east London; and secondly, knowing that this massive challenge that I had set myself over three years ago before I reached the age of seventy was now complete. I would now have to fester at home and set myself another, hopefully not too daunting challenge, to manage my increasing old age.

Acknowledgements

I am, once again, greatly indebted to Allan Buxton, who has produced the excellent route maps which accompany this narrative. Also, to Bob Lawton whose excellent cartoons light up this book. As before I would like to thank all those people I have met on my travels who have provided material for this, my fourth walking companion guide book of Kent and East Sussex. Finally I would like to thank my daughters Jessica and Eleanor (known as Ellie) for their encouragement and my long-suffering partner Wendy for her patience and support in this ambitious project.

Correction

On page 22 I wrongly suggested that the improved section of the A 21, effectively by-passing Southborough is known as River Hill. This is not the case as River Hill lies south of Sevenoaks on the original main road, now the A225. This hill involves a climb northwards up the steep slope of the Greensand scarp face. Nethertheless my father would have been impressed by the greatly improved route of the A 21 but I doubt whether he would have wanted to cycle along it.